MALA: A STRING OF UNEXPECTED MEETINGS

Paul Mason learned the practice of Transcendental Meditation when he visited Maharishi Mahesh Yogi's *ashram* at Rishikesh after hitchhiking to India in 1970. He has maintained an abiding interest in India and has produced a fair few books relating to the teaching of meditation.

Titles by Paul Mason

Maharishi Mahesh Yogi: The Biography of the Man Who Gave Transcendental Meditation to the World

The Beatles, Drugs, Mysticism & India:
Maharishi Mahesh Yogi - Transcendental Meditation - Jai Guru Deva OM
Roots of TM: The Transcendental Meditation of Guru Dev
& Maharishi Mahesh Yogi
^
Den Transcendentala Meditationens Ursprung - Turning Pages
Swedish edition 2017

108 Discourses of Guru Dev:
The Life and Teachings of Swami Brahmananda Saraswati,
Shankaracharya of Jyotirmath (1941-53) - Volume I
~
The Biography of Guru Dev:
The Life and Teachings of Swami Brahmananda Saraswati,
Shankaracharya of Jyotirmath (1941-53) - Volume II
~
Guru Dev as Presented by Maharishi Mahesh Yogi:
The Life and Teachings of Swami Brahmananda Saraswati,
Shankaracharya of Jyotirmath (1941-53) - Volume III

The Knack of Meditation:
The No-Nonsense Guide to Successful Meditation

Dandi Swami: The Story of the Guru's Will, Maharishi Mahesh Yogi, the Shankaracharyas of Jyotir Math & Meetings with Dandi Swami Narayananand Saraswati

Via Rishikesh: A Hitch-Hiker's Tale

Mala: A String of Unexpected Meetings

Kathy's Story

The Maharishi: The Biography of the Man Who Gave Transcendental Meditation to the World
Element Books - First English edition 1994
Evolution Books - Revised English edition 2005
Maharishi Mahesh Yogi - Aquamarin - German edition 1995
O Maharishi - Nova Era - Portuguese edition 1997

Established in Yoga, Perform Action:
Gita Bhavateet; The 'Song Transcendental' of Acharya Satyadas

MALA
A String of Unexpected Meetings

★

Paul Mason

PREMANAND
www.paulmason.info
premanandpaul@yahoo.co.uk

This edition, revised and updated
Published by Premanand 2020

© Paul Mason 2004, 2006, 2012, 2013, 2020

All rights reserved
No part of this book may be reproduced
or utilized, in any form or by any means
electronic or mechanical, without
permission in writing from the Publisher.

All images copyright Premanand
Cover design by Premanand

ISBN 978-0-9562228-6-2

'MALA: A String of Unexpected Meetings'

An account of an inspirational visit to Rishikesh, India

There comes a time in most people's lives when they feel a need to get away for a while, take a break, have a rest, get refreshed and revived. And most of us dream, daydream, of having an easy carefree holiday in some exotic location. But usually we don't get around to it, as we neither find the money or the time, nor are we decisive enough to fulfil such wishes, but settle instead for a treat or a weekend trip.

When we do actually allow ourselves to have what we think we deserve, we most certainly don't know how things will unfold, whether things will go according to plan, or even that we won't end up regretting our decision.

Anyway, a plan is hatched; a few weeks in India, just resting and topping up the batteries, recharging, and rebooting, no sightseeing or racing about…

Chapter 1

Gods, *gurus* and Bollywood film idols gaze down from paper posters hanging above the market place. Brightly coloured bunting and shimmering tinsel decorates the shops and market stalls of Rishikesh. Throngs of people roam about, and all over town the crack, report and tremor of fireworks sound throughout the day and night.

The main road is lined with every conceivable trade and filled with honking trucks, buses, taxis and swarms of buzzing motorcycle auto-rickshaws, all belching fumes. Rishikesh is no longer the quiet holy town of old, which has drawn truth-seekers for countless generations.

With only a few days to go before the Hindu New Year, preparation for the celebration of *Divali* (the festival of lights) is in full swing. Interested in the festival, though I am, the town is too noisy, dirty and busy for my taste.

With a view to finding accommodation on the other side of the river, I walk the long busy road that leads out of town.

After about half an hour on the main road, I take a byway on the right, which leads towards the riverside.

Avoiding direct eye contact with beggars who line the route, I make my way through the jostling crowds towards Ram Jhula, a gently swaying narrow pedestrian suspension bridge which spans the clear rippling glacial waters of the River Ganges. The '*jhula*' ('bridge') was built recently to provide a ready link to the opposite shore, a picturesque community crammed with temples and *ashrams*, lying at the base of rolling tree-lined hills. The village there is called Swargashram 'Heaven Ashram' and has for centuries been associated with the lives of saints and sages. Faithful pilgrims flock to Rishikesh on their way to the various temples and shrines in the Garhwal Hills - the 'Land of the gods' - and nowadays the area of Swargashram is very popular, frequented by truth-seekers and tourists alike.

Religious institutions offer overnight lodging and it is easy enough to find cheap accommodation in an *ashram*, which serves as a religious guest house, such as Ved Niketan, a pretty russet-pink, white and yellow building sited on the bank of the Ganga River. Over the years this facility has given shelter to many, and as the donations have flowed in, the buildings have expanded. These days, visitors are asked to abide by a rigid code of conduct:-

> **Residents must take a decision to adopt virtue and give up vice.**
>
> **Here it is compulsory to get up at 4am and do some meditation and regular exercise after cleaning the body.**
>
> **It is a must for all inmates to attend the prayer meetings held from 6am in summer and from 7am in winter.**
>
> **Use of onions, garlic, meat, fish, eggs, liquor, hashish, bhang, biris & cigarettes etc. is strictly prohibited.**
>
> **Playing cards, chess, chowser, radio and unsocial activities, political discussions, cutting jokes, undesirable gestures, reading dirty novels - Strictly Prohibited.**

I realise I would probably receive a good welcome at the *ashram*, but my wish to avoid any conflicts regarding rules is strong enough reason to consider finding somewhere less proscriptive. Frankly, I have no intention of adopting a routine to awake at four o/clock in the morning on this long awaited vacation.

As it happens, I received an unexpected cash gift before leaving for India, to make sure I got 'comfortable' accommodation. The gift came from Yolanda, with whom I had previously hitchhiked to India & who must therefore remember how uncomfortable life on the road can be.

Though there was once a time when accommodation in a religious institution was all that was available to visitors here, nowadays several enterprising businessmen have moved into the area and set up guest houses and hotels for those wishing for something more than a simple monastic cell. I want to lie on something softer than a concrete shelf and on this trip I am eager and willing to sample the delights of easy living, Indian-style.

I decide to look for a cheap hotel.

Having located a suitable hotel, in the midst of Swargashram village – the Green Hotel - a clean, attractively painted and modestly priced facility with good views of the Himalayan foothills - I notice a group of guests seated at the rooftop restaurant, so I ask them how they rate the hotel. A young woman voices her opinion: -

'Although the rooms are nice enough, I guess, it is most definitely not quiet here. There are children shouting all the time outside. Just thought you might like to know. Huh?'

'Mmmm. Thanks. Perhaps I'll look at some other places before deciding.'

To locate some of the competing hotels one only has to follow the local signs throughout Swargashram village, there are a few others to choose from, the Rama, the Sudesh Guest House and the Hotel Rajdeep. Fortuitously, as I search the right one, an opportunity to glean more information is afforded by a chance encounter with a young Australian woman at Hotel Rajdeep. I recount the warning I have so recently been given, whereupon she fixes me with a steady gaze and responds breezily:-

'Well, if the noise bothers you here, then come to my room and I'll teach you how to meditate!'

I smile, wondering whether or not to correct her, as noise is of no particular concern to me, except perhaps whilst meditating, when some sounds can become a bit intrusive. Still, it is nice of her to offer me meditation tuition.

Chapter 2

The following day I check out of my room in Rishikesh and with rucksack hung loosely hung over my shoulder, wander down to the main road and turn left, northwards out of Rishikesh.

'Ram Jhula?' queries the driver of a black and yellow *phat-phat* motor rickshaw taxi.

'Yes, *Han Ji*,' I assure him, 'I go Ram Jhula then to Swargashram.'

Climbing into the motor propelled rickshaw I edge myself into the cramped cabin of the three-wheeler and sit down, my bag between my knees.

I nod a greeting to my fellow passengers.

'*Namaste*,' comes the response from an Indian man, with a red *tilak* on his forehead, who has probably just visited a Hindu shrine or temple.

'*Namaste Ji*,' I respond.

'Where you are coming?' he asks me.

'England.'

'Oh good, good... You are liking India?'

'Yes, it is friendly here. More friendly than England.'

'Good. Good. You want *sigrat*?' he offers. 'No?' he asks again, cupping his hand round a lighted match then blowing a plume of cigarette smoke from the corner of his mouth.

Of a sudden the vehicle lurches forward; making me grab and grip tight the tubular steel roof support. Then we head off along the busy street with our driver feverishly sounding his horn as he overtakes rival motor-rickshaws and hastens onward, only occasionally slowing to stop and let fresh passengers aboard before speeding on noisily. It is almost impossible to make conversation above the sound of the engine as we hurtle towards the fuel pumps and old temples of Muni-ki-Reti, and past the various spiritual missions that abound here such as Yoga Niketan and Omkarananda Ashram. Finally, as we near the riverside drop-off point near to Sivanand Ashram, the *phat-phat* brakes suddenly and with difficulty I clamber out of the confined space.

The driver drops the *rupee* coins into the pocket of his torn grubby shirt and smiles giving a flash of his stained, yellow, gapped-teeth before wildly accelerating again, and pulling away in a cloud of exhaust fumes.

I now make my way along the path that leads towards the foreshore of the Ganges, Unlike my last visit, this time I intend to cross the river by ferryboat, so purchase a ticket and wait on the steps for the boat.

I sit on the steps of the *ghat*, alongside some Indian pilgrims and look out across the gently flowing waters, enjoying the view of the waterside *ashrams* and the gentle hills beyond dotted with temples. As I soak up the gentle sights and sounds around me for a few minutes I find myself cured of any impatience to be on the move.

From amongst the few hotels I visited the other day I am inclined to stay at Hotel Rajdeep, for it is very well-positioned, nestled as close to the jungle behind Swargashram village and with a commanding a wonderful view of the surrounding wooded Sivalik hills. I am met at the reception.

'Yes sir, you want luxury room?' asks the manager, a friendly well-mannered bespectacled old gentleman with the bearing of one whom has in all probably seen a certain amount of military service. He gives me an inquiring frown that causes his thick-rimmed spectacles to rise up on his nose.

I soon learn that in addition to providing standard accommodation (with optional bucket of hot water) the hotel also offers luxury rooms with deep pile carpets, comfy upholstered armchairs, balcony and ensuite toilet facilities complete with hot and cold running water and shower.

'How long you are staying sir?' the manager inquires.

'I'll be in India for several weeks more,' I offer.

'You are using air-conditioning?'

'No. I don't need it.'

'Then I can give you very good rate.'

'But can I use the fan?'

'Of course!'

I take to this man easily, not least because he allows a substantial reduction on the room rate.

'You are paying for how many days, Sir?' he asks solicitously.

'Initially, I will pay you for ten days.'

'This is good. You have passport? I see?

I get out my passport and pass it to him.

'If you will wait a few minutes everything will be completed.'

Whilst he is involved completing the paperwork, I cast my eyes about the hotel foyer, casually scanning the various advertisements that adorn the walls and windows, which inform of the various classes and activities available locally. My musings are interrupted by a request for me to sign the visitors' register. My passport is returned, along with a receipt for the prepaid rent.

The hotel manager now accompanies me to my room, and tells me his name, which is Chaturvedi. His name indicates that he comes from a line of Vedic *pandits*, scholars who commit ancient religious texts to memory. Abashed he admits he does not carry on the tradition.

Nonetheless, I soon discover Chaturvedi Ji is a man of words, and wants to talk about books, and then he suddenly scurries away. I wait for him to return and fill my time emptying the contents of my small rucksack. He soon returns with a quantity of books clutched to his chest. He seems to have a great love of literature, a passion he wants to share. He thrusts several paperback books at me; one is entitled *'Are You Experienced'*, a novel about travelling about India. Another is a bulky fantasy novel by Terry Goodkind, which Chaturvedi Ji seems really keen for me to read.

'I would like to know what you think of this. Myself I found it very interesting,' he booms.

'Okay, but have you any books on Indian philosophy?' I ask.

'Don't worry for those,' he responds gruffly, 'this book here is very good, very much imagination. You very much will like.'

'I can't promise to read it all,' I say, 'but I'll give it a go', I assure him, and he is off again, beetling out into the outside corridor.

*

After finding suitable places for the few possessions I carry with me, I settle down on the bed and prop myself up on two cotton-filled pillows, and begin reading the fantasy tale. It tells of an innocent in possession of a magical stone, who becomes caught up in the machinations of a series of sorceress queens. Curiously, whilst I read, a suspicion dawns on me, I figure that maybe I am fated to read these very pages, that they are some sort of a warning, for me to be on my guard.

Though the book is well-written and reasonably absorbing, I lay it down after only a few chapters, perplexed that after coming all this way to India I have been persuaded into spending my time lying here in an upmarket hotel in a holy village in India, exploring a Western author's over-ripe imagination. Instead, impulsively, I decide to venture outside, with the intention of having a wander through the shaded jungle reaches close by.

The day has by now become very hot and is somewhat humid too, so I make sure I take a supply of fruit juice, defence against dehydration. At first I am apprehensive about exploring the thickly wooded hills alone, for reasons of safety, as I carry all my travel documents and money in a zippered wallet around my neck. Clearly, the thin white cotton high collared shirt I wear does little to conceal the bulging pouch. I feel certain that the loss of this object would usher the most unsettling of consequences, but I continue my walk, drinking in the sights of dappled leaves and smelling the scents of late blossoms.

Occasionally a hand-painted sign catches my attention and I stop to interpret its meaning. I can read Hindi, for over the years since first visiting India, I have tutored myself in the language, which at least means I can read the Devanagari alphabet and so I am able to sound any unfamiliar words in my head. Many of the signs point to Neelkanth Mahadev Mandir, a temple many miles up high in the hills, a climb I plan to take soon. For now, I content myself just strolling relaxedly. It is so-o-o good to be away from the incessant commotion that has surrounded me these last few days.

It's been some years since I visited India last, though in my heart I never left, However, this time, when I emerged from Delhi Airport onto the street outside, I found myself totally unprepared for the intensity of India's power to shock and strip me of my self-assuredness.

The bus ride from the airport into the centre of Delhi was an unexpected test, quickly turning into an act of faith, for there was simply **far too much** chaos going on, inside the bus and outside too. I made a discovery, that chaos is what I most fear, and since arriving it seemed that everyone and everything turned this power to perplex me. Admittedly, I had expected a bit of hassle on my arrival, but not the total all-pervasive pressure I had to endure. It had made me seriously re-evaluate my decision to take a break here in India. But now, in the wonderfully verdant jungle, away from the mayhem, I am feeling far more relaxed.

Wafting along the dusty tree-lined way, listening to the caw-cawing sounds of the busy black jackdaws and crows, and the twitter and trill of exotic birdlife, I catch occasional glimpses of the gentle long-tailed black-faced bearded *langur* monkeys who live here, some playing with their young in the branches that overhang the track.

At length a large archway comes into view and to the left of it a path leading up a temple, Bhutnath Mandir, and to the grounds of the grand bright pink and white multi-storied structure of the Kailashanand Nature Cure Centre, someway high up the hill. I am tempted to take a closer look at the place, but since it means climbing up a long steep path, I figure it can wait until another day. Instead, I decide to take the easier route, which gently leads towards Dhyan Vidya Peeth, and on the way I occasionally pass some horned cows and oxen that roam freely throughout the jungle.

It was near here, at Dhyan Vidya Peeth, the Academy of Meditation, that back in the spring of 1968, many of the world's media descended in pursuit of The Beatles whose taxis lumbered along this very track after bumping, grinding and honking their way from Delhi, when they came to visit the *ashram* of Maharishi Mahesh Yogi, the 'giggling *guru*'.

A journalist asked Maharishi:-

'Some people think of you as a saint, what is it that you preach?'

'I teach a simple system of Transcendental Meditation which gives the people the insight into life and they begin to enjoy all peace and happiness. And because this has been the message of all the saints in the past they call me saint.'

'You seem to also have caught the imagination of the pop stars?'

'You mean The Beatles,' he giggled. 'I found them very intelligent, and young men of very great potential in life.'

The Beatles, along with their entourage and a few other celebrities, joined the dozens of long-term meditators wishing to become teachers of meditation. The course ran for many weeks with all participants attending lectures, and putting in extended periods of meditation, with participants eating in the communal canteen and enjoying impromptu concerts from the resident artistes and visiting Indian musicians.

Beatles George Harrison and John Lennon & Mia Farrow
with Maharishi Mahesh Yogi, sitting by the Ganges, at Rishikesh, February 1968

Swami Satchidananda, Maharishi & Tat Wale Baba, Rishikesh, April 1968

And there were other visitors to the *ashram*, neighbours such as 'saints', and in particular one known at Tat Wale Baba who appeared to be only in his forties, though it is said that even then he was at least one hundred years old! He was a popular local dreadlocked holyman of some renown.

Transcendental Meditation (TM) first gained prominence in the late 1950's after Maharishi Mahesh Yogi embarked on his first world tour. In this system of meditation the student is advised to set aside about twenty minutes twice daily in order to relax quietly and loosely focus the mind on a selected *mantra*, a calming, soothing sound that assists the mind to go beyond thought. The TM technique is taught worldwide and, if correctly practised, brings about a state of restful alertness. It is claimed that, with regular practice, a state of 'Cosmic Consciousness', a condition of illumination or enlightenment, can be attained.

These day the training courses for TM teachers are conducted elsewhere, as Maharishi Mahesh Yogi no longer visits India. Quite a long while back, and without explanation, western visitors were denied all access to the *ashram* site. It is rumoured that the Indian Government had detected a security threat amongst foreign visitors, suspecting some of them to have been spying for their respective countries - an unsubstantiated but intriguing rumour.

I chance upon an overgrown path to the right and pursue it, believing it to lead to the *ashram*. At length, after treading the path for several minutes, I come to a cluster of derelict huts beside which is a wide rusted iron gateway hung with jaunty makeshift wooden gates, fastened, chained and padlocked. Drawing closer, I peer through the gates into the *ashram* grounds, my gaze following the line of heavily damp-stained, formerly whitewashed, chalets, opposite which stands a large residential block. I can't be certain, but all the buildings appear completely deserted.

As I stand there waiting and looking for some sign of life, I still can't be sure whether there is anyone about. But nothing seems to stir other than butterflies in slow flight and birds moving from tree to tree. Then, a lone cow slowly ambles into view. I stare for a time and am prompted to speculate on how the cow might have entered the enclosure. A strong urge to take a closer look beyond the gates arises in me, I want to get through them and explore the grounds. To this end I hit on a notion, to simply follow along the perimeter wall and hope to find a breach in it.

I search about, and discover traces of what appears to have once been an established path, but it has long since become overgrown. As I stumble along, the thick undergrowth really impedes my progress and the outgrowing branches keep blocking the way. Undaunted and fully immersed in the challenge, I press on giving scant attention to the long-spiked thorns as they snag my clothes and sink into my skin causing my flesh to bleed. The scent of the many orange and pink blossoms is faintly intoxicating. Amongst the foliage, spiders the size of one's hand are lurking, and portions of their sticky superstrong webs tenaciously cling to my hair. Quite suddenly I become anxious - I sense the presence of something moving closeby.

Cautiously, I step forward as silently as possible. I can still hear the noise somewhere ahead. I am within a few feet of it when suddenly I discover I come face to face with it, a stray ox grazing in the thicket - and I sigh aloud with relief.

Tempted as I am, to scale the high moss-lined walls of the *ashram,* in order to gain entry, I resist, reminding myself that if a cow can find a way in without needing to shinny up the wall, so can I!

Continuing on my way through the undergrowth, I eventually emerge from the thick foliage into a rough stony gorge. It is a massive relief that, for a while at least, I no longer have to fight my way through the jungle.

I carry on though, and follow the dried up watercourse for some yards before coming in sight of an ornate gateway to the lower entrance of the *ashram*. Disappointed, I note that these gates too are locked. How exasperating! I am by now dirty, tired, disappointed and really at the point of giving up, when I discern a slight gap in the wall to the right of the grandiose gateway. Without hesitation I step right through it, climb up the steep bank and enter the *ashram* compound proper.

The grounds here are filled with trees, and the area is intersected with broad walkways, providing a tranquil and pleasing place to wander. There still appears to be no one else about, so, cautiously, I begin to explore the overgrown *ashram*, getting right up close to the buildings, derelict and sprouting greenery from cracks and fissures – there are bushes, even trees growing out of some of them.

The few signs and signposts dotted about give evidence to the former occupancy of the site. I stand and stare at one in particular:-

महर्षि कुटिया

The hand-painted metal sign nailed at the beginning of a tree-lined path informs that the building beyond is '**Maharshi Kutiya**'. I follow the path and come to a large squat building, this *'kutiya'* (or *'kutir'*) is no mere hut or cottage, (as the name might suggest), but an impressive looking residence designed and built back in the mid-1960's for Maharishi

Mahesh Yogi himself to live in.

I have visited here before, in fact I was taught the technique of meditation known as Transcendental Meditation, also known as TM, here, many years ago, after I had hitch-hiked from Great Britain to India via North Africa and the Middle East, with my girlfriend,

I knock at the door of Maharishi's *kutir*, but there is no reply. I check the door down there to see if that is open, but alas that too is closed up. It was down in the basement meditation room that I was taught TM. I then move across the pillared terrace area to survey the abandoned lawned garden, which I then walk around, passing the disused water features and I contemplate the interesting varieties of shrubs and mature trees there.

Just beyond the bungalow, at the brow of the hill, I sit myself down and take some shade beneath the trees, enjoying the breathtaking view out across the river Ganga. I sit there relaxing, this is a very special place.

Of a sudden I realise I am not alone.

A tall, well-built, unshaven Indian gentleman attired in white high-collared *kurta* shirt and loose white *pyjama* pant trousers walks towards me. He stands peering at me quizzically.

Self-consciously I volunteer a vague explanation:- 'Hi, I'm just taking a look about.'

'I am staying below, I come to walk also.' he pants breathlessly, beads of perspiration dripping from his forehead, 'What your country is?'

'England.'

'You are liking India?'

'Here I like, it is very peaceful.'

'Yes. I before here am coming.'

'I wanted to meditate downstairs, in the basement.'

'I think it is locked. I think there is *swami* staying here.'

'He is with the Maharishi's organisation?'

'No.'

I am intrigued as to who it is who has installed himself here, but beyond that he has already told me, he appears to be able to add nothing.

'So, for how long has the *ashram* been empty?' I ask.

'Two years? Maybe two years? Yes!'

'But why is it empty?'

'It is this... Mahesh Yogi here no longer is interested. He now big place in Europe has.'

'But why leave all the buildings to go to waste?'

'They rent not have paid. So... government is coming in... Government everything is closing down. If rent they not pay, what to do?' he asks.

'But they must be doing something about it.'

'No, nobody here comes, just they are writing something, maybe.'

'But I'm sure they can afford the rent,' I puzzle.

'You before I am telling, Mahesh Yogi no interest has! No.'

'Oh well, at least we can enjoy the peace here.'

'In Hindi language the peace is *shanti*, very much *shanti* you take in India, my friend,' he calls cheerily, then disappears suddenly, off down the path.

I linger after his departure in order to sift through a pile of mouldering papers I have spotted lying in the garden. On closer inspection I find that they are fairly neatly stacked, sets of blank forms printed in Hindi and in English, for use in checking the progress of novice meditators' experiences. Only recently could they have been placed there, else the wind would have blown them far and about, so I am puzzled how and why these documents relating to the teaching of this system of meditation have so unceremoniously been dumped amongst the parched and wilted flowers of Maharishi's *kutir*.

It is quite moving to have returned to this place, a place where I was taught to transcend thought, encouraged to find that special inner peace which is said to be our the natural birthright. But the shadows are getting long and it is high time I return to my rented room.

*

Back at Hotel Rajdeep, I set to work trying to remove jungle stains from my shirtfront. In the event it proves to be a greater task than I had imagined. I apply yet more soap, followed by yet more rubbing and persevere until I'm interrupted by a tapping at the door.

It is the henna-haired young woman I spoke to the other day, who tauntingly offered me meditation tuition.

'I'm looking for a woman who left me a message...' she explains distractedly.

'Oh!' I respond.

Self-evidently I staying here alone, so the link to the whereabouts of this woman who left the message remains unexplained. Notwithstanding, I feel I need to excuse my dishevelled appearance, so I point out to my visitor that I have been roaming about in the jungle and that I'm trying to remove the stubborn green stains from my clothes.

She appears quite unmoved by my ramblings, and just remains still, standing framed by the doorway, her almond shaped eyes staring ahead with a fixed expression. From her manner it appears she is looking at something inside my room. Actually, I imagine that she is making an extra-sensory sweep of my personal space, and taking an inventory.

'You can come inside, if you like,' I offer, rather belatedly.

My words appear to signal an end to her contemplation - indeed, they seem to provide her a spur to action.

'I should go and find this woman,' she muses thoughtfully, but still she does not move, just standing still contemplating

Then, of a sudden, she whisks away, and shoots off down the corridor, leaving me standing, bewildered. I resume my laundry work, but somewhat distracted by the question as to why the young woman just happened to knock at **my** door.

***

The hotel has several floors and a flat roof, from which the entire area can be viewed, a great vantage point from which to observe the domestic life of the local villagers. I notice that atop of their simple low dwellings are haystacks, presumably foodstuff for their animals, and here and there, growing between the homesteads, are fruit trees of mango, guava, fig and banana.

To the front of the hotel, on the same floor as my room, is an open-air terrace area dotted with tables and chairs, where guests can partake of snacks and meals as an alternative to eating in the restaurant on the ground floor.

One evening, after having stayed at Hotel Rajdeep several days, I feel inspired to sit awhile at the rooftop café and very soon I strike up a chat with a hirsute ginger-haired Canadian chap, who sits draped in a brightly coloured poncho, contentedly playing a semi-acoustic guitar. Occasionally he stops to mark down the notes he is strumming. He confides to me that he is currently pursuing an interest in 'music therapy'. I don't mention it, but actually I don't know quite what that means, therapy for whom, him or someone else? I assume he means for others. My interest though is with his guitar.

'I have a very similar guitar back home, an Indian acoustic - cello-style,' I comment.

'Right!' He smiles.

'But your guitar's got a much sweeter tone to it.'

'Oh! Right. Yeah.'

'I prefer to play electric though, I like to make a noise!'

'R-i-g-h-t!'

Happily absorbed in the flow of his thoughts and music, he appears to have but meagre appetite for conversation. Though he speaks very little he is nonetheless enjoyable company. Even so, when I notice the still seated shape of the mystery lady gazing out into the evening sky, I sidle over to join her at a table close by. We've encountered one another several times over the last few days, as I've scuttled back and forth to the shops and taken walks in the warm sunlight. This seems a good opportunity to get better acquainted and I start to tell her of a recent trip I have taken, to a temple in the hills called Neelkanth Mahadev Mandir, a temple dedicated to the god Shiva.

'On the way up there,' I tell her, 'I saw a group of about fifty *langur* monkeys lunching on one banana tree.'

'Huh!' she responds.

'Lord Shiva is something of a local lad,' I continue, 'Apparently it was at Neelkanth that he drank the poison that turned his neck blue, hence *neel* - blue, *kanth* - throat.'

'Oh I haven't heard of it before. Is it close?' she asks.

'No, it's quite a long climb, but you can get a shared jeep which is reasonably cheap. Neelkanth temple is very beautiful, though initially I passed by on a different path and found myself at a different temple further up the hill which is where I got this,' I explain, as I point to the red cotton bracelet on my right wrist, 'It's supposed to protect my health!'

As I talk I study the expression on her face; she appears to be totally self-absorbed. From her countenance an almost preternatural light radiates from her eyes and from her skin. I imagine I sense shifts of colour about her face and hair (a trick of the light perhaps).

She tells that though she has been livng for about twelve years in India, she has never before visited Rishikesh. Apparently, until recently, she has been living in Manali. Then she felt drawn to journey to nearby Dharmasala, the seat of the Dalai Lama, the exiled Tibetan Buddhist spiritual leader. But instead of going to Dharmasala she travelled several hundred miles in the opposite direction, and found herself in Rishikesh.

I listen to her in with a feeling of suspended disbelief, as her explanation makes it sound as though she took no active part in making the journey. But I make no comment, and she goes on to explain how since arriving two weeks before she has been teaching various spiritual practices.

'Nirmoha is my *sannyasi* name. *Nirmoha* means, "free from illusion",' she informs me.

I feel inspired to guess that Nirmoha is likely connected to the 'Orange People', the community in Poona founded by the late Bhagwan Rajneesh.

The coloured light display about her brow continues to dance as she speaks of many things, in particular she stresses the importance of imagination. This reference to imagination prompts me to mention the magical fantasy book the hotel manager has lent me. I give her a rough idea of its content, highlighting that the story tells of a sorceress and a magic stone.

'Why waste time on someone else's imagination when you can have your own?' she demands, somewhat contemptuously.

'Well, as it happens, I have a problem with imagination! Personally I much prefer to deal with reality.'

'But imagination is everything!' she states categorically, 'Everything is in our imagination!'

Oh! The conversation is suddenly getting very 'deep', and I choose not to get drawn in, so I let the matter drop. But I'm curious that she has said nothing in response to the mention of magic, for I suspect this is where her real interest lies.

After sitting awhile, Nirmoha raises a new topic, reffering to a practice I am unfamiliar with by the name of 'Reiki'. I have a feeling it is probably a martial art with a zippy name. I ask her directly: -

'Why should I get interested in some Japanese sounding thing then?'

This display of crude ignorance and its attendant attitude seems to surprise her. In consequence she appears to buckle for a few moments but then she soon bounces back.

'Ian can tell you about it!' she says, pointing across the terrace to my newfound guitar-playing friend, 'He has just completed a course with me. Let him explain Reiki to you!'

At this point Nirmoha rises to leave and slips away, out of view.

So, I rejoin Ian and, interspersed between further bouts of his guitar playing, we discuss the various reasons that have brought us to Rishikesh. I confess that though I have no clear reason, beyond wishing to relax, I entertain vague hopes that it would be nice to meet and network with inspiring people. I share my conviction that I believe it's possible for as few as a dozen or so individuals networking together to be able to trigger huge social changes. He listens patiently, interestedly.

And when I bring up the topic of Reiki, Ian willingly offers to share with me something of what he has learnt on the course with Nirmoha. He describes a process involving the laying on of hands.

'But how can anybody possibly heal someone merely by touch?' I query.

'One can become a conduit or channel for the Universal Life Force,' he explains. But whilst the words flow from him I somehow doubt that the thoughts are his own. Indeed, to my ear, the ideas sound suspiciously pre-digested, And despite Ian's best efforts, he can offer no scientific explanation to support his claim, so I am left with the impression I am being told of magical practices. When I put this idea to him he appears unsettled as he reflects on the implications of this assertion.

Ian and myself talk long into the night and as the hours pass the warm air turns chill. Ian seems to be fighting the symptoms of a head cold, and he wraps himself tightly in his poncho. I decide to go off and order more tea, and so I wander off, and go downstairs. In the foyer I find Chaturvedi, he is with someone called Ashwin, who I am told is the boss of the hotel, both of them are watching cable colour television. But, at my appearance, the TV is turned off.

'Come, let us talk,' invites Chaturvedi Ji.

They attempt to draw me into a philosophical discussion. As I sit, I wonder whether Chaturvedi and Ashwin get on well.

'This is my father,' Ashwin tells me, placing his arm affectionately around Chaturvedi's shoulders.

'You are very lucky,' I tell him.

'Yes, but why you say that?'

'He is good man.'

'But, how do you know this?'

'Sometimes just feeling is enough. I sense he is good.'

'But you don't know!'

'Yes, I do, I trust him, that I know.'

'Why do you come to Rishikesh? What is it that attracts?'

'It is spiritual place. It's good to be back.'

'Before you have come?' Ashwin enquires.

'Yes, years ago I hitchhiked to India from England, through Europe, North Africa, Turkey, Iran, Afghanistan and Pakistan. But coming to Swargashram, it was **so** peaceful.'

'Now it is very different?'

'It was less busy then. But it is still good. I feel I have come home again,' I admit, sighing contentedly.

Ashwin eyes me in silence for several moments before announcing:

'I am business man, I have many problems.'

'Then you should listen to your father, he is in business but also he is interested in spiritual matters.'

'But I have too many problems, how can he help me?'

'Because he is not so caught in problems.'

Just then Ian makes a brief appearance to bid 'good night'. I am tempted to make my exit too.

But it is much later, about two o'clock in the morning, before I prise myself away from a great debate and return to my room. I then reflect a little on my chat with Ian, remembering how he had, by way of explaining about Reiki energy, taken hold of his thigh between thumb and first finger and then described the sensation of the flow within.

I feel inspired to test his description and so I begin trying to emulate his actions. The experiment proves a resounding success for I soon begin to detect the flow of energy, it is just as Ian describes!

Chapter Three

The realisation that I have only slept for about three hours does nothing to discourage me from arising early next morning to greet the new day. And after meditation and a light breakfast I take to the lanes that lead towards the Ganga with the idea of walking up alongside the river this morning.

Traders in Swargashram are just now opening up their shops; and some of the stallholders have already started to neatly arrange their colourful wares. The scent of sandalwood oil hangs in the air. There is a mood of calm, an easy friendliness in mutual greetings. Those children fortunate enough to have places in school proudly make their way there carrying books and lunchtime snacks. They call out to me: -

'How are you? From what country are you coming?'

They crowd about me, and I speak to them in simple Hindi, they to me in simple English.

'You speak very good English,' I tell them.

Their faces light up and they start giggling, laughing and chasing one another about.

'Have a nice day,' they shout, running off and turning round to repeat their well-wishing, waving until out of sight.

I continue walking, and descend a short slope where many beggars have already begun to congregate.

'*Hari Om*,' they call out cheerfully.

I nod and smile.

Coming to the village post office, I stand patiently outside near the open door of the staff entrance, waiting to be noticed by one of the clerks inside. Eventually a man in a long loose *khaki* coloured shirt spots me and indicates in a vague way that he will be with me shortly. At length he moves over to the counter and starts to sort out his desk.

'*Dak* tickets, for postcards,' I request of him.

He flickers his eyebrows whereupon he wordlessly responds, first by opening a ledger, and then, slowly and methodically he sorts out an appropriate combination of stamps to fit the current rate of international postage. I pay the clerk, and after checking my change get busy affixing a number of stamps and airmail stickers to postcards I wish to send. Then, thrusting the cards into the jaunty domed bright-red sheet-metal pillar-box, I let forth a sigh of satisfaction. Job done!

As I make my way to the waterfront, I pass the nearby eating houses and street vendors selling snacks. I press on making my way towards Ram Jhula suspension bridge. Along the side of the river, pilgrims are gathering on the *ghats*, the steps that lead down at the waters edge, where the visitors bathe and anoint themselves with the crystal clear chill holy waters of the Ganga. A mood of holidaymaking pervades the air. The bathers smile and laugh to each other as they refresh themselves and sing their prayers. Up on the gently swaying bridge walk the beggar children who attempt to sell handfuls of small doughballs to visitors in order for them to feed the vast shoals of huge glistening golden *mahseer* fish that wait expectantly in the still waters below, hoping soon to be showered with blessings from above.

Instead of crossing over the bridge I instead turn to the right of the bridge and continue on along the riverside path, enjoying the sight of the many varieties of flowering shrubs along the way. Walking towards me on the pathway comes a group of pilgrims and with them a monk, clad in very bright orange cloth. He strides quickly towards me and immediately attempts to strike up conversation. He is unaware, of course, that I have consciously decided to avoid getting caught up in the machinations of *sadhus* or zealous *ashramites*.

'You are coming from which country?' he asks, fixing me with an unusually intent expression.

I smile but say nothing.

'Please, I wish to speak with you!' he states insistently.

I continue walking, and ignore his questions; concerning country, name and so forth. He isn't easily put off and keeps trying to get my attention, so I turn the game around a little and ask him a question instead. I try to elicit from him the order of monks he is connected to, for there is something oddly familiar in his look. I know what it is; he bears a strong resemblance to a particularly eminent religious leader, Swami Shantanand Saraswati, the Shankaracharya of Northern India. Not only do I recognise the same roundness to his cheeks, the generous bleach-white 'Santa Claus' beard but also most importantly the resemblance is strongest in his soulful compassionate eyes.

'Come, come, we can find a place to sit down and talk,' he says. 'You are wanting to drink tea?' he asks, as we pass a *chaay* vendor. 'Come. Come here, he is soon bringing tea for us.'

Chaay? Well that does it!

Finding a quiet spot to sit, with the intention of settling down on some steps leading to the river's edge, to wait for the *chaay wala*.

'So, what do you want to talk about?' I ask him directly.

'You are in a hurry. No hurry there is. We can sit and drink tea together, it will be good!' he reassures me. Then he sets an example by making himself comfortable, sitting himself down crossed-legged.

I gaze at the *sadhu*, at the scarlet and vermilion markings on his broad forehead. Suddenly he wrinkles his brow as he shades his eyes from the bright sunlight. I study his facial expression but cannot easily fathom it; a curious mixture of breathless earnestness and an almost childlike innocence.

Again he attempts to question me, but I interrupt him: -

'First, tell me something about yourself,' I demand.

'My name is Shiva Balak, I am in Allahabad for three years. There I am studying Sanskrit at Brahma Nivas.'

'Really! At Shankaracharya Swami Shantanand's Ashram?' I ask suddenly excited.

'Yes.' He says, surprised. 'You have been to Allahabad?'

'No, but I would like to! I did visit Joshimath monastery some years ago. I am very interested in Shankaracharya Shantanand Ji's *guru*. I have read his life-story. He was very, very great soul I think.'

'This is very good,' he comments thoughtfully.

I explain to the old *sadhu* a little of my own spiritual quest; as I do so the old man leans over and grasps my forearm.

'You are *guru bhaiee*, my *guru* brother.' he exclaims. 'I must give you another name, *sannyas* name.'

Gazing at me for some moments and sweeping his hand from side to side he solemnly proclaims: -

'Premanand! Premanand is your *sannyasi* name; *prem* is love. *anand* is bliss. Premanand! Premanand!'

Though I am certainly no *sannyasi* (for I have not taken, nor do I wish to take, vows of *sannyas*, of renunciation), I feel blessed to be given this name. And, as it happens the word *anand* has for years been one of my favourite Sanskrit words.

'And I must write for you *mantra*!' he says excitedly, 'This *mantra* you must hear!'

First of all he speaks some words of the *mantra* (in praise of the god Shiva) and then writes them down, in the Devanagari script with its sharp lines, curves and flourishes.

He then sings them to me with clear and sonorous voice: -

गांगा तरङ्ग रमणीय जटाकलापं

गौरी निरन्तर विभुषित वामभागम् ।

नारायणप्रियमनङ्गमदापहारं

वाराणसीपुरपतिं भजविश्वनाथम् ।

gaaMgaa tara~Nga ramaNiiya jaTaakalaapaM ,
gaurii nirantara vibhushhita vaamabhaagam .
naaraayaNapriyamana~NgamadaapahaaraM ,
vaaraaNasiipurapatiM bhajavishvanaatham .

I believe this '*mantra*' is in praise of god Shiva, lord of the *yogis*, translated it reads: -

'The one whose matted hair resembles the beautiful waves of the river Ganga,

Is eternally adorned with Gauri (the goddess Parvati) on the left part of his body.

The one dear to Narayana (god Vishnu), the one who punished the ego of Madana (the god of love),

Lord of Varanasi, Lord of the Universe, I sing of you.'

We chat a while longer, during which time I share with him some of the dried mango fruit I carry with me. We continue talking until I notice we have attracted a crowd of spectators around us.

Shiva Balak loudly and very publicly announces to the onlookers his assertion that he and I are '*guru* brothers'. It is clearly time to move on, so I start to inch my way up the steps in a bid to get away. Shiv Balak loudly protests but I take my leave anyway, delaying only to leave him a small cash gift, a contribution towards the cost of his beloved Sanskrit books.

Alone again, I pursue the sandy path that twists its way to the next village, which lies a couple of miles upstream. First the path hugs the banks of the holy river Ganga, then becomes a sandy track which meanders past the simple dwellings of various local holymen.

Here in these *kutirs* live several monks, *swamis* belonging to religious orders such as Giri (mountain), Aranya (forest) and Saraswati (goddess of Wisdom) who have taken *sannyas* (vows of non-attachment to possessions, chastity and obedience to the head of a religious order). It is said that *swamis* generally avoid sensory indulgence, but this is not true of all holymen. For many *sadhus* the smoking of *ganja* (cannabis) is common practice. Confusingly, both *swamis* and *sadhus* wear the cloth of orange to mark them apart from the rest of the community. It is usually quite easy to spot the resting-place of a holyman for there is often found to be hanging from a tree or fence, pieces of orange cloth hung to dry. The orange colour can range from washed-out faded pink through any shade of ochre to highly saturated near-red hues.

In one of the huts I pass lives the 'monkey man', and catching sight of me, he walks directly towards me. His arms are stained with coloured dyes; his face is daubed with crimson face make-up. Following behind him swings the appendage of a fake tail. It is to be assumed that he is seeking to evoke the memory of Hanuman, the devoted monkey helper of Lord Rama, who for many devout Hindus is seen to embody the twin virtues of humility and service. For me though, the theatrical monkey man who is blocking my path symbolises no such qualities. He demands my attention with a menacingly hiss, and by the waving of his mace. Placing a fingertip of orange paste on my forehead he greedily demands a large amount of money with hisses becoming steadily more intense the longer I withhold payment to him. Eventually, I give in, and give him something!

'*Hari Ram*,' he growls.

The path I have taken from Swargashram eventually joins the pilgrims' roadway leading to the busy village of Lakshman Jhula. The story of the building of the *jhula* (bridge) is linked with the god-king Lord Rama of Ramayana fame, who allegedly visited Rishikesh with his brother Lakshmana. Allegedly, when Rama desired to cross the river, Lakshmana took an arrow to which he had attached to a hank of rope, and shot it from one side of the river to the other, across which the brothers clambered safely to the other side. So, Lakshmana's improvised 'bridge' is believed to be the predecessor of the modern suspension bridge, the steel construction that exists here now. This story of the god-man Rama is not the only local story of note, as it is also believed the area is connected with the famous Pandavas, the five sons of Pandu, named Yudhisthira,

Bhima, Arjuna, Nakula and Sahadeva. The brothers were contemporaries of Lord Krishna and feature prominently in the epic poem *'Mahabharata'* and are said to have stayed in a cave a little further upstream from here.

Lakshman Jhula village, like so many places these days, is expanding at an alarming rate, with hotels, *ashrams* and temples competing for any available space to build and expand. Every day crowds of pilgrims flock here enroute to and from the shrines of Badrinath, Kedarnath, Gangotri and Yamunotri, high in the Himalayas. The pilgrims' needs are anticipated by local businesses which sell recordings of devotional music, pictures, statues and pendants of saints and gods, incense and coloured powders for making paste marks on the brow. Moneychangers, gem shops, grocery stores, cafes and restaurants have positioned themselves adjacent to the most popular *ashrams*. Every few yards along the way are stalls selling *chaay* (tea which is boiled rather than brewed) and snacks. Other stalls offer cheap gifts; bangles, badges, necklaces and combs. I inspect one of the well-crafted wooden souvenirs, and find it reveals a hidden surprise; the box has a concealed snake that bites the finger of the unwary. Though the snake may not be real, the pain is real enough!

Having no reason to delay any longer than necessary at Lakshman Jhula, I decide instead to return to Swargashram in order to look for a remedy for the persistent cough I have brought with me from England. I don't even stop for another *chaay* but get into my stride and take the broad path, slowing only to watch the antics of *langur* monkeys I see on the way, climbing about in the trees. I pause occasionally to greet a stranger, placing palms together in *Namaste* greeting. '*Namaste*' is said to mean 'I bow to the spirit of God within you!'

Once back in Swargashram I purchase a return ticket for the ferry and am soon cruising across the broad Ganga River towards the Shivanand Ashram. Near the main *ashram* there is a Ayurvedic Dispensary, which sells many preparations made from local herbs; products such as 'Brahmi-Amla' oil that 'cools the brain and eyes', 'Netra Jyoti Surma' that 'imparts brilliance to the eyes', and 'Chyavanaprash' of which it is claimed 'develops memory and strength'.

But as soon as I arrive a stranger accosts me, and after but a few minutes of company, announces; 'I will come and visit you at your home in England. I know this! You may be surprised at my certainty, but that is how it is!'

He appears to be Indian but his accent is European, or at least it appears so when he speaks to me, but when he stops at a stall nearby, in order to buy a padlock, his fluent Hindi, spoken with North Indian dialect, tells a different story. In English he tells me his name is Giri Maharaj, that he and his wife have travelled from Finland - where he officiates at ceremonies - and that his brother is a famous local writer. Giri informs me too that he is currently occupied in researching the availability of holiday property around Rishikesh.

I listen to Giri without making comment for something troubles me about him. His manner is just way too intense. However, after listening to him a while, I feel I should say something, and I'm moved to share the news of my new name. I begin my story; 'For years I have wanted an Indian name. Why only last night I thought about it and lo and behold, this morning a *swami* gave me ....'

'You want Indian name?' He interrupts. 'I give you one. Mmmmm, yes, I've got it ... Atmaram. Your Indian name is Atmaram.'

'But, I was just trying to tell you. I now have an Indian name - Premanand.'

'Oh yes, Premanand, yes yes. Means the same. Premanand, Atmaram, means the same thing, same thing,' he states assuredly, in a rather dismissive manner.

It must be time for me to try to extricate myself from his company, so I tell him I must go, on the pretext that I need to return on the next ferry.

'You know something strange,' he confides, moving uncomfortably close up to me. 'Even though I come from this very area and many times I have come and gone over this river, I have never once travelled by ferry.'

I am minded to think that this leaves a sizeable hole in his story, bearing in mind that Giri is middle-aged, and the bridge was built less than 25 years ago, so, if Giri has known this place since he was a kid, wouldn't he have visited the area before the bridge was built, when the ferry was the only option?

Aboard the ferry I opt to keep conversation with Giri to the minimum and once I am safely across to 'my' side of the river, I made a bid to wish him goodbye. At that moment we are close to one of the village's two music shops and he is now pointing excitedly at a boxed set of recordings of Osho Rajneesh, which is displayed there.

'Now there's a man worth listening to!' He asserts with particular gusto.

I eye Giri with suspicion, sensing that he is trying to draw me closer, possibly with the intent of drafting me into his belief system. I know something of Osho and his teachings. It is said he dropped in on one of Maharishi Mahesh Yogi's teacher training courses once, in Kashmir, in 1969.

In one of Osho's innumerable publications, entitled *'Anything Can Be A Meditation'*, the charismatic cult leader offers his opinion that 'meditation is all about de-automization'; 'Walking, walk slowly, watchfully. Looking, look watchfully, and you will see trees are greener than they have ever been and roses are rosier than they have ever been. Listen! Somebody is talking, gossiping: listen, listen attentively. When you are talking, talk attentively. Let your whole waking activity become de-automatized.'

I decide to leave Giri there, still pointing at the cassettes and CDs. As I have by now decided to leave the purchase of the cough mixture until another day, I walk past Choti Wala, up the hill past the sprawling *ashram*, and along the footpaths back to Hotel Rajdeep.

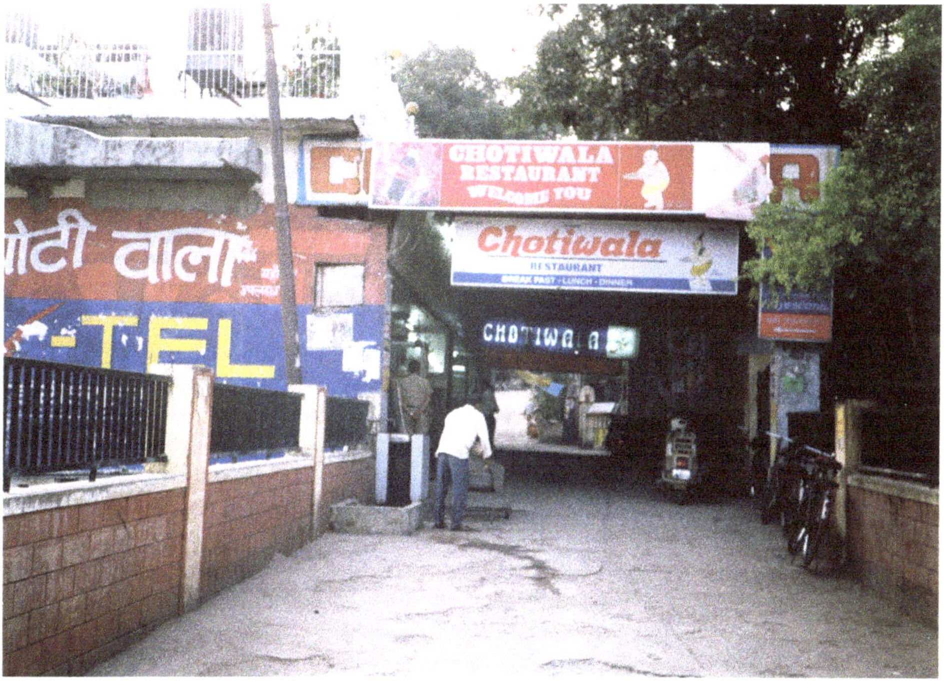
CHOTIWALA
RESTAURANT
WELCOME YOU
Chotiwala
RESTAURANT
BREAK FAST · LUNCH · DINNER
CHOTIWALA

गंगा दर्शन

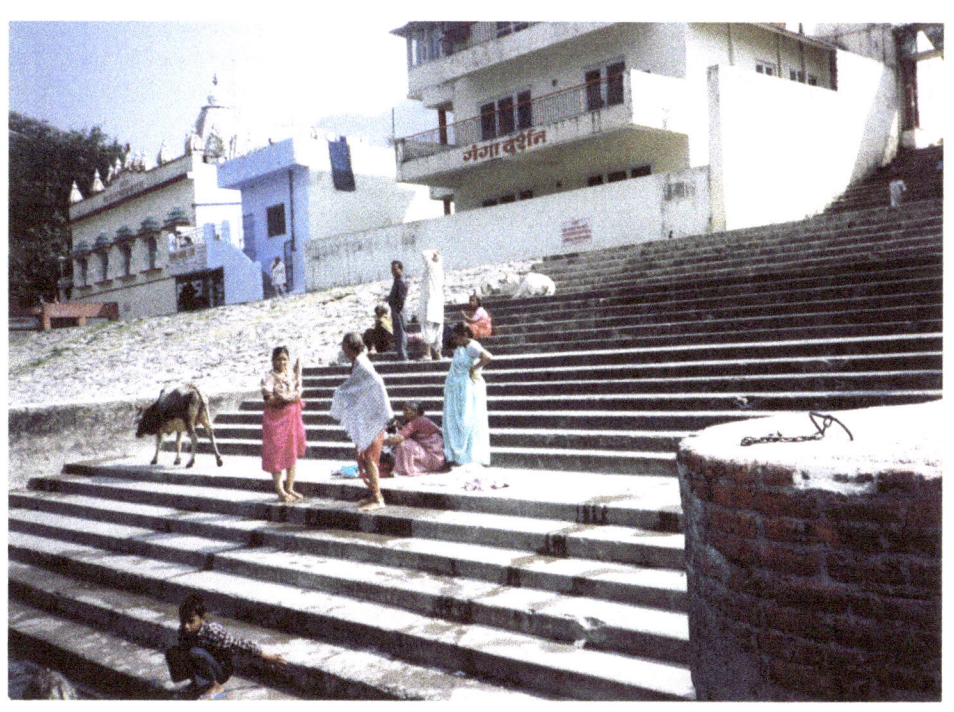

In my experience, the winter climate in India, during October and November, generally outstrips even the best of English summers. So, this is reason enough to take every chance to get out and about in the hot sunshine during the day. Even in the evening it is still very warm and I find it is most pleasant to read, write and relax out on the hotel terrace. The cultural diversity amongst the guests makes for easy conversation often stimulating, sometimes fruitful. Travellers tend to tell tales, exchange news and express views. Why, even talking about the weather can take on surprising depths when one is seated with a French meteorologist.

Several guests have lately joined a *hatha yoga* class; practicing on the flat roof of the building next door. Afterwards, in the evening, they slump down in the seats beside me in the rooftop café, exhausted from their efforts trying to perform their *asanas* correctly. Tonight it is Sadie's turn; she collapses down sweating and tired. She has clearly been overdoing it.

'In Hindi *asan* means easy,' I tell her, 'so, if the *asanas* aren't easy, then perhaps they should be. Why not take it easy?'

I intend my remarks to be helpful and supportive., and fortunately she doesn't misinterpret them.

'That's just what I needed to hear!' she says, brightening considerably, 'Thanks.'

She sits there puffing and panting, and when she speaks again she still sounds a bit breathless.

'If you don't mind, I think I'll go and lie down for a while,' she says.

'Good idea. See you around.'

I continue to sit on the terrace, and I spend time writing up some notes. And Ian and Nirmoha soon join me. The news of my '*sannyas*' name causes Nirmoha to chant; 'Premanand, Premanand, Premanand. Now you must call yourself Premanand. Yes. Premanand, Premanand, Premanand,' she enthuses. 'Actually,' she adds quietly, 'Prem is my name too - Prem Nirmoha.'

I am puzzled. If the name she has been given is Prem Nirmoha, which means 'love without attachment', why has she shortened it to 'Nirmoha', which just means 'not attached' or 'unattached'?

As with our previous meeting, Nirmoha and myself now fall into easy conversation, and as before the colours again dance around her hair and brow. Try as I might I cannot find an explanation for the colour shifts, but since she seems such a positive individual I do not feel threatened by her personal magic. However, when conversation returns to the subject of Reiki, I find she still seems totally unwilling to explain what it is. I wonder why. Then she astonishes me completely, announcing in a self-assured, almost prophetic, way: -

'Maybe you stay here and teach Reiki!'

I am dumbfounded at her presumptuousness! I have no inkling at all as to what the teaching of Reiki entails, so why on earth would I want to teach it? Besides, I have no intention staying in India beyond the few weeks scheduled. But before I have time to summon up an adequate response to her, she has risen from her seat and slipped away, leaving me alone to contemplate her words, and to gaze at the starry sky and listen to the sound of night birds.

I get up and join Ian, who listens attentively as I tell him of my conversation with his Reiki teacher.

'She's a very powerful woman!' I announce. 'She worries me!'

Ian does not respond.

'With that sort of power...' I continue, 'well, I just hope she uses it wisely.'

'I don't know what you mean exactly, but I'm listening,' he says slowly.

I tell him of the colours. I also explain to him that I suspect she is trying to use the power of autosuggestion to influence me. He seems astonished to hear that she has mooted the idea of my becoming a teacher of Reiki, though less surprised that she believes I might stay in India, reminding me I have already indicated I am not entirely satisfied with life back in England.

'Ah, but I never said anything about stopping in India!', I protest.

Sitting huddled in his blanket and wrapped in thought for a time Ian eventually breaks his silence and offers to share a few insights into the course he has recently taken with Nirmoha.

'Well I'll just tell you what comes to mind. I don't know if any of what I can say will be of any help though. Here goes anyway. First off, she played 'trance' techno-music at the sessions. Oh, and in the corner of her room is a shrine with a photograph of Osho, and some tarot cards on it.'

'Okay, that's useful.'

'Oh yeah and she's really into semantics.'

I had also noticed how for Nimoha certain words had very specific meaning, so much so that I felt discouraged from offering any alternate interpretation.

Ian continues; 'I also found her 'teacher' manner surprising.'

'How do you mean?'

'Well I really didn't expect it.'

'Tell me more.'

'Well there was this one time when I guess my attention had wandered, and she really startled me. I suddenly found her staring at me. It was then that she asked me; "Where are you? Where are you, right now? Where are you?"' he recounts. Clearly, he is still bristling with indignation, even at the recollection.

'Okay. Anything else?'

'Yes, we were doing this meditation exercise, and there was the sound of a child crying nearby.'

'And..?'

'Well, I figured there might be something wrong. So her indifference to the sound of the kid's suffering unsettled me.'

'But that's meditation, sounds come and go.'

'Yes, but you still care don't you?'

'I know what you're saying.'

'Anyway, that's it, I can't think of anything else.'

'So, what did she make of **you** Ian?'

'She congratulated me on being a 'good listener'.'

I instantly recall that in the fantasy novel I have been reading, the central character is called the 'Listener' and he becomes similarly worried, about the issue of lack of emotionalism in the woman he meets who seems to have a magical influence on him.

Ian and I chat deep into the night and we turn our attention to all sorts of topics, such as Ian's music therapy studies and his nostalgic affection for his drinking buddies in Canada. He also brings me up-to-speed with his travel plans, telling me that he has booked a ticket on tomorrow's train for Varanasi. All at once, stressfu impressions of my recent journey to Rishikesh spill out into my mind.

*

Delhi is no longer just a bit too busy and materialistic; it seems to have developed an ominous energy. The numerous craters in the road, the many neglected grimy buildings and the ruins all seem to scream of impending doom and certain annihilation of living, breathing life - pollution is not a mere concept here, it assaults the senses so completely, swathing all in a blanket of noxious vileness. The vehicles all seem unroadworthy, and no driver seems in control, despite their determined expressions and the manic glints to their stares as they drive about in mad frenzied animation.

The desire to curtail my visit had very abruptly and forcefully asserted itself, but commonsense told me not to change my ticket at such short notice since this airline only undertakes one flight a week. No, the second best idea that I was able to extract from my embattled thinking process was to press on in the hope that things would be better beyond the city.

Once across Delhi I booked a seat on a 'luxury non-video coach', a vehicle seemingly cobbled together from scrap parts and it's 'air-conditioning' was supplied by the open windows and passenger door. It took more than an hour to leave behind the sprawl of poverty that extends around the capital, but thereafter I glimpsed trees, occasional fields and, intermittently, small rural villages with thatched huts, cattle, and cow-dung pancakes piled high in conical heaps, ready for use as domestic fuel. There are many towns too, where, and as the coach slowed down, children climbed aboard, desperate to sell their wares of fruits, nuts and sweetmeats, whilst others passed their goods through the windows to those that proffered the few *rupees* called for.

*

So, I really don't envy Ian the three-day journey ahead of him, even though his forthcoming trip, by train and buses will eventually take him to the famed hippy Mecca of Katmandu. Before he leaves, Ian writes down his e-mail address, and his 'proper' address in Canada. We vow to stay in contact, as so many travellers so often vow to do after touching briefly on one another's lives.

Chapter Four

Only recently have I come by a clue as to the possible title of a treatise I have been in search of, containing no less than 112 techniques for transcending thought, of turning off the thinking mind. After a moment's hesitation standing outside the window of one of the village bookshops, I step in and test my luck.

The shelves are stacked high and display a bewildering array of titles, a vast wealth of spiritual literature. The shop assistant looks at me expectantly.

'Do you have a *tantrik* book called *Shiva Sutra*?' I ask.

'What you are wanting? Many *sutras* there are!'

'It is called something like *Vaighan Bhyghan Tantra*.'

'You want *tantra* book?'

'Yes, the *Vaighan Bhyghan Tantra* of Lord Shiva.'

The assistant smiles deeply, strides over to a bookcase and plucks out a thin red paperback, which he holds up for me to see. Its cover is illustrated back and front with beautiful coloured prints depicting Lord Shiva and his consort.

'*Vijnanabhairava*,' he announces.

With barely suppressed anticipation I open the volume and glance at the subtitle; *'Divine Consciousness - A Treasury of 112 Types of Yoga'*.

'Yes! This is the book I want. Brilliant!' I exclaim.

I purchase it immediately and once outside the shop cannot restrain myself from sampling its contents. Soon my mind is swimming with the suggested practices considered as *'yoga'* which can best be illustrated by a quote from the book, Verse 72 reads: -

'When one experiences the expansion of joy to savour arising from the pleasure of eating and drinking, one should meditate on the perfect condition of this joy, then there will be supreme delight.'

I suppose that many actions can be considered as *'yoga'*, perhaps wandering could be said to be a *yoga* too, taking life as it comes, witnessing the day unfold. Here, in this holy village, in this peaceful environment charged with the aspirations of so many truth seekers, treading the paths trodden by saints, sitting on the shore of the Ganga river on sand possibly touched by enlightened *yogis*, it is easy to allow time to float out of mind and just enjoy the now.

My walk brings me to a brightly painted statue, one that depicts a Hindu story of creation, peopled with gods and semi-divines. The goddess Lakshmi attends her consort, the god Vishnu, as he reclines on a huge multi-headed serpent, Ananta Shesh. From Lord Vishnu's navel springs the lotus on which is seated the god Brahma, looking out to all four directions. Facing Lord Vishnu, with palms placed together, stands the eagle-like divine bird Garuda and also attending are the Gandharvas, divine musicians depicted with the heads of horses.

Turning from this splendid statue, I walk on past a local landmark, the clocktower, the face of which has the hours marked in Devanagari numerals. Close to the tower, by a small temple, there sit a couple of glazed-eyed young *sadhus*, with ringletted long dark hair tumbling about their faces and onto their naked torso's. They puff eagerly at their tapered clay *chillum* pipe of sparking, smouldering cannabis.

Walking on further along the shore downstream; after a few minutes I find myself on the outskirts of the village, at the *ashram* of Ved Niketan (Palace of *'Veda'* or 'Knowledge'), somewhere I have stayed several times in the past. I pause here, wondering if I might spot the house-*guru* basking out in front of the *ashram*, as is his want. But today he is nowhere to be seen, so I continue walking along the soft sandy path beyond the *ashram*, past the thatched sunshades of the adjacent eatery, which appears to have discontinued business. I turn off and out onto the broad beach which slopes gently to the river.

Continuing on my way slowly, I arrive at the base of the hill of Shankaracharya Nagar, and notice that on a nearby wall monkeys are sporting about ,and as I watch them I'm caught by the thought of taking another look at the deserted remains of the Maharishi Mahesh Yogi *ashram*, it is such a peaceful spot.

On this occasion I decide to seek out a more direct path than that which I had taken on my previous visit. But no sooner do I start walking towards the hill than a voice rings out, challenging me; 'No, no. You cannot go there,' shouts the agitated voice.

I swing around in order to identify its owner, and am relieved to find no menacing representative of authority, just a figure attired in long *khadi* (homespun cloth) shirt and *lunghi* (loose cotton cloth draped about the legs). He stands beside the entrance of a makeshift hut of sticks and tarpaulin. He doesn't appear threatening in the least, but it occurs to me that he might be employed to guard the local vicinity.

I eye him steadily as I try to take control of my temper.

'I have already been up there to the *ashram*, now I am looking for a new path,' I tell him - I assure myself that the steady tone of my voice betrays no indication of my annoyance.

As it happens, he shows no interest whatsoever in my response but instead invites me to sit down and drink coffee with him. Somewhat grudgingly I accept his offer, and he sets about dragging out two blue moulded plastic chairs from within his hut.

'What do foreigners get from coming here?' he asks me abruptly.

'I don't know,' I state honestly, then I turn the question around and ask him: -

'What **do** they get?'

He appears shaken by my response, and he rises and shuffles about uncomfortably before steadying himself sufficiently to offer his thoughts on the matter.

'I think this. I think that they feel better about themselves after seeing what state are the people here.'

Clearly he has already given the matter deep consideration, which is much more than I have done.

'Maybe they do, I really don't know,' I answer simply.

In silence he disappears inside the hut, presumably to prepare our coffee. As I sit alone it occurs to me that this man might hold a clue to a local mystery.

I call out to him; 'Can you tell me something? Why is the Maharishi's *ashram* now deserted?'

He emerges quickly; seemingly ready to offer me his opinion.

'You have attachment there. I do not!'

The utter simplicity of his words surprises me, as does his command of English.

'Yes, I suppose I do have attachment,' I answer honestly, 'But have you ever been up there, to the *ashram*?'

'I have no attachment. I do not go anywhere,' he states.

His manner is unsettling; to say the least, especially after I discover that any new line of conversation is met with similarly dismissive responses. I change tack and ask him about himself. With this line of enquiry I fare a lot better discovering that he comes from Bangalore and I am surprised to learn had been employed as a computer programmer. He tells me he has travelled to England and visited the birthplace of William Shakespeare at Stratford-upon-Avon. Chatting with him and sipping scalding hot instant coffee, from a stainless steel beaker, I begin to feel a bit more comfortable in his presence, comfortabe enough to share with him a few details of my own life. I then ask concerning his family, whereupon he stiffens very noticeably but he does not hesitate in giving an answer: -

'Yes I was married with family. I was sole survivor of crash,' he announces.

I am taken completely off my guard, and stunned by what he has just told me. It is a long, long while before conversation resumes between us. Then Rameshwar Das starts to explain how for the past three years he has dwelt beneath the spreading Banyan tree, existing solely on unasked gifts given by anyone who might come to see him. He tells me that he walks no further than the waterfront of the Ganga, and then only in order to wash and to obtain drinking water. He also tells me of the conditions inside his living quarters informing me how snakes sometimes come to share his hut.

'If they bite me I die,' he announces resignedly, shrugging his shoulders.

I wince in discomfort.

'I do not fear them,' he continues, 'I think more that they fear me,' he says, without a trace of emotion in his voice.

Rameshwar's unworldly attitude inspires me to try and discover what teaching, if any, he follows. But my mention of *swamis* and *sadhus* elicits no more than a disdainful look, and he gets up and goes once more inside his hut. I join him and watch as he rummages amongst his few belongings. Eventually he produces a dusty old book, which he passes to me

'I think this book it is very hard to find now,' he says proudly.

I leaf through it, but it appears quite ordinary, a fairly standard primer on *yoga* exercises.

'Thank you for showing it to me,' I say politely as I return it to him

By now my coffee is finished and, as we have talked for quite a while, I figure it must be about time I was on my way. Before leaving, I ask Rameshwar what he would like me to bring him, if I were to return this way again. He answers evasively; 'If someone brings me food, I eat. If drink comes, okay. If no food comes then I don't eat.'

'But what do you need?' I persist.

'If there is food I eat. If there is nothing, it is all the same.'

I reflect that during our conversation he made mention of a cassette radio he once owned – that it had needed mending and he had given it to someone to take to Rishikesh. When the machine was not returned, even after many weeks, Rameshwar took his few cassette tapes and laid them at the waters edge; 'I offered them to Mother Ganga,' he explained.

I now ask him; 'Would you like a radio?'

'If you bring, fine. If you don't bring, fine too.'

'You're impossible, you really are impossible' I tell him.

As it happens, I am irritated at his apparent pretence at equanimity, for I am convinced his philosophy is a sham, designed to mask his pain. I detect that beyond his words, beyond his philosophy of unattachment, lurks plenty of unfulfilled desires. So I try further to wheedle out of him some idea of what he might want from me, but he maintains a stoic silence, that is until I get up to leave. Hesitantly he confides to me: -

'Well, it would be nice to have radio here, for company.'

As I retrace my steps along the path back to the village I reflect on enigmatic Rameshwar's outlook on life and ask myself why he has abandoned responsibility for himself by settling himself in such a lonely spot with so little chance of anyone knowing of his plight? I wonder what has made him so determined to do nothing to better his lot? Despite his great loss, surely he too needs to follow the maxim that 'God helps those that help themselves,'' the idea seems equally applicable to all. Now, if he were a monk of some kind it might be different, such eccentric behaviour is somehow easier to understand in someone of a reclusive nature, but Rameshwar had been a family man.

When later I tell others of Rameshwar's predicament they all appear sympathetic, and when I tell Nirmoha she surprises me in that she apparently finds his story inspiring; 'He sounds really interesting. When are you going to see him again?'

'I don't know if I will!'

'Oh but you must. It's not far is it? Go on!'

'Maybe. Maybe I'll get the radio for him. Maybe not.'

*

I visit Rishikesh market the following day, though it is not to look for a radio but to change money at the State Bank of India, a process that involves no less than three clerks and a protracted wait. Whilst in town I search for a detailed map of the area, stopping by a bookshop where I find myself browsing local guidebooks and self-help tutors of every description. One particular teach-yourself book catches my eye. It claims to offer the complete knowledge of Reiki healing, including how to become a Reiki Master. Impulsively I purchase it.

On my return to Swargashram, I chance to meet with Nirmoha, outside the Choti Wala restaurant. When I mention my purchase of the Reiki book she eagerly seizes the volume and begins scanning its pages.

'Oh no, no, no. They have included the symbols,' she exclaims frowning, then remains absorbed in thought before adding; 'they have the symbols wrong, they should not have included them at all. These things should not be placed in books. The teaching of Reiki should only be learned from a qualified Reiki Master not from books.'

I gather from this that I am being discouraged from reading the book, and that I am being guided to enrol in a class, her class, but, as yet, I still feel unwilling to commit.

*

Although absorbing and fascinating, interest in people, interest in things, and interest in ideas, can all be sources of distraction and create unrest sometimes. In order to feel more fully refreshed I find it is often necessary to be totally alone for a while.

The countryside remains a place where alone we can confront our hopes and fears. The sights, sounds and smells of nature have the power to restore flagging energy and refresh ones senses.

The local jungle around Rishikesh is no longer quite the wilderness it once was, for the flow of buses, trucks and jeeps on the newly cut asphalt road is definitely not conducive to the well-being of the animals, but the area still contains much wildlife. Though large wildcats are rare, it is not uncommon to come across deer, monkeys and peacocks.

'Sir, I am asking you not to walk on jungle side after eight o'clock,' requests Chaturvedi Ji, the hotel manager.

'Why is that?'

'Elephants sometimes coming in darkness! Elephant most dangerous animal!' He warns darkly.

In point of fact, apparently, up until a few decades ago, the only serious recorded crime in the area is said to have been occasioned by an elephant, which is said to have strangled someone.

Despite the real and imagined dangers, I am determined to turn my back on people for at least a few hours, and so I set off on another trek.

One reason I am drawn towards the leafy jungle groves is that by wandering in the jungle, I might meet with a *yogi* or some other hermit who might be dwelling there. For time out of mind truth-seekers have resorted to jungle hermitages in order to find their answers. Amongst the Indian Scriptures, it is the *Upanishads* that contain the wisdom of such jungle dwellers. One translation of the Sanskrit word *'upanishad'* is that it means 'to sit near'. Within these *Upanishad* texts are many accounts of those who came in search of enlightenment, for the desire to become happier is natural, as is the wish to obtain greater clarity about the purpose life. It seems only few find lasting happiness and enlightenment without help.

Today it becomes evident that I am not alone here, for along the way, stationed at close intervals, are soldiers, here to protect teams of athletes competing in a fitness-training programme! It is an unlikely coincidence, the army turning up on the same day as my big walk, and it causes me to postpone the hike. But perhaps I too am in need of protection here, and if I don't venture far from the sight of the posted sentries, I too will enjoy their protection, I guess?

*

Recently, Nirmoha offered me the chance to listen to a recording of *satsang* (spiritual meeting) with an American woman, Ganga Ji, who is said to be enlightened. I gratefully accepted the opportunity. I now discover this interesting woman speaks her truth softly, patiently, almost mesmerically, in fact, but seemingly with utter conviction:-

'The greatest challenge is to let go of all understanding. I'm not suggesting you cling to misunderstanding or not understanding. Let go of that as well,' Ganga Ji advises.

She sometimes quotes her *guru* (whom she calls Papa Ji), who states:

'If you touch it, it will bite you!'

As I listen to the tape, I wonder how to interpret the words beyond their most obvious meaning. Both Ganga Ji, and her *guru*, Papa Ji, appear to be warning us not to underestimate the power of the exterior world, not to underestimate its power to unsettle our inner stability.

Ganga Ji states that 'It' is ever-present, 'It' is the reality we all seek to find, and as such, 'It' never was, 'It' never ceases to be, 'It' always 'Is'. By constantly reminding her audience of this, and other truths, she seemingly hopes to affect a material change in their capacity to enjoy their lives. Intent on instilling a mind-set of increased awareness through self-enquiry, she encourages everyone to live in the present and not to become distracted by self-created stories and excuses concerning imagined limitations, brought on by events of the past.

'Honestly, let's say the event happened. It did not happen the way you remember it happening. That's the truth. Actually the event didn't even happen, but I'm not asking you to go that far! And I'm not asking you to deny your memories. I'm asking you to see what's deeper.'

Ganga Ji inspires adulation. A young man reports to her; 'I woke up one night and I had this hit me, that I was just like you.'

'That's right. That's right,' her velvet tongue reassures.

'And I thought it was so arrogant, at first.'

'It's arrogant to think you aren't!' she counters.

'Yeah!'

'That's right. That's right.'

'So my time's coming?' he asks.

'You're turn is here!'

She adds; 'You're time is not separate from my time, and it's not separate from Ramana's time, or Buddha's time, or Christ's time, Mohammed's time, or all the unknown awakened beings in all realms, in all degrees of form and formlessness. Same, same. It is arrogant to think otherwise and this arrogance is the cause of much unnecessary suffering.'

To another man, George, who had written to her asking for a private meeting, she summoned him to sit on 'the private cushion' and talk with her before the entire assembly.

Ganga Ji advocates complete surrender to 'Grace'.

'The truth is continual surrender. This is the challenge of this experience of incarnation; this is the joy, the victory. Victory is surrender.'

Her speech is extremely direct; 'Maybe you have been very foolish in the past, or maybe you have been very wise. So what? Right now, how are you spending your time? Where is attention? Where is surrender? Where are you?'

When I next open my eyes I discover that, although I have only recently been listening to Ganga Ji's encouraging words, the tape is no longer running. Actually, it appears that many hours have passed. Indeed the light of dawn has arrived, with its uplifting glow now filling my room.

*

It has been several days since my meeting with Rameshwar and today I find myself drawn to paying him another visit. As I near the imposing and aged Banyan tree near his hut, with its dangling tendril branches, I look about for Rameshwar. He is nowhere to be seen so I call out to him, but there is no reply. I listen intently and convince myself I can detect the sound of a muffled voice coming from within the hut so I shout out a greeting and pull aside the curtain door.

'Any chance of another coffee?' I ask, flinging down the plastic carrier bag I have been carrying onto his mattress, relieved to be rid of the burden. I have walked a long way today collecting the contents, gifts for him - the 10-wave band radio and the several pounds weight of fresh fruit. I'm not expecting gratitude from him, I don't even wish for it...

Rameshwar is seated and on my arrival stirs uneasily, telling me; 'Night has been bad. Epileptic. Now you are here I am feeling much better. But, cooker... now not working.'

'Can I help?' I volunteer, leaning over the bed to get a closer look at his cooking area.

But it is clear he wants no help. He tries to sort things out for himself, and fumbles about without result – he seems to be in extreme discomfort.

'Don't worry about the coffee,' I assure him, 'I have some fruit juice, it will be fine.'

Rameshwar sits still, silently staring into space whilst I drain the contents of a small carton of mango juice. The silence makes me uneasy, so I wrack my brains as to how I might stimulate some light conversation. But what can I say that won't sound hollow and superficial? After all, he has obviously suffered so greatly, what with the loss of his family, his reduced circumstances, and his poor health. But I determine to break the silence anyway, but, unusually for me, I find it hard to find the words.

'When I first met you,' I start, but as I speak, my chest heaves, 'I felt that you... that you ... that ....'. Tears well in my eyes, I battle to keep my composure, 'But now ... now I... now I understand,' the sobbing words come without conscious thought. In spite of the emotional upheaval that I am experiencing, I query my words, asking myself 'What is it I now understand? Brushing aside the tears I seek an answer in the face of Rameshwar.

As I look across the dimly illuminated hut I see not the face of a suffering man, but a glowing blissful countenance. My chest convulses, my breathing is forced, tears stream down my face. But I recognise the famous personage of Baba Muktanand seated crossed-legged before me, who I know from a television programme shown some years before. Baba's devotees practised a teaching called Siddha Yoga in which, at the touch of Baba's yak-whisk, his devotees would go into spontaneous movements such as involuntary shaking, sobbing and sudden deep breathing.

As I gaze at Baba, I find myself backing out of the hut and into the bright sunlight, where I attempt to pull myself together. The chest spasms and sobbing continue unabated. I dab at my eyes with the sleeve of my shirt. With my vision a little clearer I look about me, and to my surprise find myself to be in the company of a lone cow who has parked itself close to me, gently flicking its tail.

Rameshwar emerges from his hut and looks at me smilingly. We exchange but few words before I tearfully bid my leave of him whereupon he gently offers reassurance saying: 'Now I feel much better since you and the cow have come to visit.'

The visit to Rameshwar at his simple hut between the jungle and the riverbank leaves me very fragile. It is as if an aspect of my body has been torn open. Those people who believe in the existence of *chakras*, seven spiritual centres aligned down the head and body, might be tempted to suggest a *chakra* had been opened. Whatever it is that has happened to me, I sense it to be a positive spiritual experience, since I have felt elated for most of the time since visiting Rameshwar. But whatever happened to me affects me deeply. My emotions now frequently churn and often, whether I'm on my own or in company, I find myself sobbing for no accountable reason.

By evening time I find myself unsure as to what to do with myself. I even contemplate leaving Rishikesh, and I phone a friend in Britain.

'You have dialled incorrectly. There is no such number,' a pre-recorded female Indian voice states repeatedly. I check the digital display panel on the telephone cubicle wall – it confirms that I have dialled the number correctly.

I give up on the telephone, and instead return to my hotel room to settle down and meditate. This smoothes me out considerably, and afterwards I decide to go and take some food on the terrace.

From the terrace I hear the sound of dance music, it seems to be coming from somewhere in the hotel, and then I recall that Chaturvedi mentioned to me that he was organising a party, a 'Gods Dancing Party'. I trace the sound of pounding music upstairs, but before taking the last few steps to the roof, I pause to enjoy the sight of petals strewn about the top of the staircase.

There is a blissfulness in the moment that is so totally reassuring, and all the troubled feelings of emotional upheaval, that I've been experiencing of late, seem to shift and subside. I enjoy the evening immensely.

Chapter Five

The new day is a good one, full of sunshine and birdsong – how great it is to be here, in comfort, right next to the jungle. It really is thrilling!

'Aha, here I am finding you!' Chaturvedi Ji exclaims, apparently glad to have located me on the hotel terrace. Accompanying him is a smiling young western woman who I have not seen around before.

'This is lady coming from Britain,' Chaturvedi booms.

'I suppose you want me to tell her what a good hotel this is?' I ask, grinning at them both, then after a moments reflection declare resolutely, 'Well, I like it here.'

Susan shakes my hand with a firmness and strength unusual in a woman.

Chaturvedi Ji continues; 'When Susan is asking to me concerning local trekking, I am thinking she must meet with you. So I am coming to look for you.'

'Maybe I can help!' I say, addressing myself to the young woman. 'With this gentleman's assistance I recently got hold of a detailed map of the area. I haven't done any proper trekking around here yet, but I'm sure I can point out a few good paths to take.'

'If you can spare the time, maybe we could chat?' Susan suggests.

'Sure, that would be nice. Right now I'm going out but we could meet up some time later? Then perhaps I could show you around.'

'That's fine with me. I've got to get settled into my room, it's downstairs, the room at the end,' she says pointing to a row of rooms to the front of the hotel. 'See you later then?'

'I look forward to it,' I assure her.

As I sit back down and leisurely finish my glass of tea, it occurs to me that since arriving in India I have grown accustomed to leaving my days open and free. This arrangement to meet up with Susan, loose and casual though it is, reminds me of just how easy it is to get caught up in other people's plans and expectations.

I am going for another walk, and once downstairs and out of the hotel I find myself being drawn again towards Lakshman Jhula. I saunter slowly and thoughtfully, desirous only to keep my own company. I ponder my mental checklist of items that friends have requested I find for them: -

1. A *mala*, a rosary-style necklace consisting of 27, 54 or 108 Rudraksha beads.

2. Two books in Hindi on the life and teaching of Shri Shankaracharya Swami Brahmananda Saraswati.

3. A herbal preparation thought to be called '*Zandopi*' or '*Zandopa*'.

4. Seeds of the *karree* plant.

Of these items only the *mala* is readily available in Rishikesh, with a wide range of choice regarding size and quality. I am dismayed that nobody has heard of the *Zandopa* powder, which is for a friend who has been diagnosed as suffering from Parkinson's Disease and he believes this Ayurvedic herbal medicine to be particularly effective at relieving the symptoms of this condition. *Zandopa* is said to be a natural source of *dopamine*, a neurotransmitter, a chemical messenger that helps in the transmission of signals in the brain and other vital areas.

I suspect I'll also have problems locating the Hindi books, which are needed in order for me to make good translations of them. One of the books tells the life-story of Shri Shankaracharya Brahmananda Saraswati who at the age of nine left his comfortably well-off family to pursue a spiritual life. It is recorded that after study in his *guru's ashram* in Uttar Kashi he was instructed to dwell alone in a nearby cave, only periodically visiting his teacher for fresh instruction. It is also said he soon found *Sat Chit Anandam* (Truth-Consciousness-Bliss or Cosmic Consciousness).

Swami Brahmananda spent much of his time roaming in jungle environments, but he was not always alone, for many sought him out to take his '*darshan*', to obtain his blessing. In the latter years of his life Swami Brahmananda's devotees eventually persuaded him to accept the exalted position of Shankaracharya (pontiff) of Jyotir Math, an ancient monastery near the famous temple shrine of Badrinath, high in the hills close to the border with Tibet and China.

I scour the Ganga Emporium bookshop in Lakshman Jhula but this brings me no closer to the treasured volumes, though Ananda, the store assistant, promises to research their availability. Whilst visiting the store I notice, amongst the many shelves displaying spiritual literature, a stack of colouring books on mainly Indian themes. A few days back I had been chatting with Nirmoha and had asked her what she had studied at university. She didn't answer me, but gave me a look as if to say 'No, maybe YOU can tell ME', so I attempted to rise to the occasion and almost without hesitation it came to me, that she is an artist. It was then that Nirmoha told me she had been doing the artwork for some colouring books, which must be the ones here in the bookshop.

I browse the books and note the volumes are credited to Nirmoha under her former name - Tania Sironic. I then read the introductory notes of a few of the works and am impressed at the clarity of the explanations about various aspects of Hindu beliefs.

The bookstore is also a café, the 'Devraj Coffee Corner', with a thatched eating area overlooking the suspension bridge. So, I settle down to sip a glass of *chaay*, and find entertainment in watching the antics of a troupe of 'red-arsed' bandit *rhesus* monkeys clambering about on the steel ropes of the bridge, looking about for a chance to ambush the unwary.

A couple - a longhaired young man, and a young woman with very short green hair - join me and introduce themselves, and sit at my table. I just have to pose the obvious question: -

'Do you mind if I ask why you have green hair?'

'Oh, we just got married!' Marianne replies eagerly (as if in explanation).

'Oh! Really? Congratulations!'

We chat awhile during which time I am surprised to find I am still prone to more outbursts of tearfulness. Consequently, I find myself sharing with them the tale of my meetings with Rameshwar.

Both Chris and Marianne appear very keen to meet with him too.

'Could you tell me exactly where we might find him?' Chris asks.

'You're thinking of paying him a visit? I don't know what you can expect...'

'Sure, these things are very personal, but, where did you say he is...? When we get through Swargashram village where the shops are, we keep on walking, right?' he asks me.

'If at first you miss him you won't be able to walk on very much further, the shore of the Ganga finishes just a little way beyond his hut. Anyway, don't worry, you'll find him. After all, he tells me he never ever goes anywhere!'

Chris and Marianne look at each other as if confirming their united agreement to go and see Rameshwar at the earliest.

'Talking to the both of you makes me think I might one day write about the meetings.'

'If you do write about your experiences, then write them as an innocent,' Chris suggests, apparently attempting to be helpful.

I try to fathom the meaning of his remark.

He appears to be suggesting that I write as though I have never before travelled to India and never before heard of personalities such as Baba Muktanand and Maharishi Mahesh Yogi.

Talking of Rameshwar has made me very emotional and I feel might be better to be alone again. So, wishing Chris and Marianne a good stay, I set off on my return walk.

About half way back to Swargashram, I observe from a distance an Indian woman with large round earrings, clad in a richly patterned orange dress, wrists dripping with gold coloured bangles. She sits cross-legged upon a rug spread out by the path, and a snake lies coiled beside her.

I hesitate, standing beside her for no more than a few moments, as any sign of interest in a peddler or entertainer is usually met with immediate demands to come, look and part with some *rupees*. So, I walk on, reflecting on the cruelty of exploiting fellow creatures for purely financial gain. But the woman's voice rents the air and I find myself involuntarily turning back and walking over to where she sits.

With her encouragement I cautiously stroke the snake, which, although appearing slimy, feels surprisingly soft, almost furry to the touch. Furthermore the snake makes no rapid movements, as I feared it might, but instead it lies still, seemingly enjoying the attention. As the woman picks up the serpent I marvel at its looped coils shimmering in the sunlight, then she leans forward to set it about my shoulders. To my surprise I do not resist, I merely witness my fear, and gradually the fear falls away. The long snake is heavy about my shoulders, but I enjoy bearing its weight. Although I don't know whether the snake is venomous or not, I convince myself it will not harm me. Many times I have seen pictures of the *yogi*-god Lord Shiva bedecked with snakes and sitting peacefully upon a tiger skin. I now identify myself with the image easily.

'I am Shiva!' I tell the woman.

'Shiva Shankar, Shiva Shankar,' she affirms nodding gently. The snake's head turns to face me, a very long tongue darting out of its long narrow jaws. I do not flinch; neither do I fear that it might poison me. When the snake is lifted off me, I happily part with a few *rupees,* which is what is expected of me, and I realise this experience has addressed a very deep-seated fear.

'Python,' the woman states smiling at me. I nod and draw myself to my feet. A group of onlookers stand about and I hear one of them say to another as he takes a sidelong glance at me: -

'*Pagal*,' he mutters. (*pagal* means mad!)

I resist the temptation to respond to his comment and instead keep my peace.

I do not very walk far up the track before I notice a young westerner guy sitting beside the path, apparently resting.

'Hi, how's it going?' he calls.

'I just had a python around my neck, its skin was so soft.'

'Snakes are beautiful, where I come from, in Colorado, we have loads of them, rattlers, rattlesnakes.'

'You don't fear them?'

'No.'

'I think animals respond to fear. If you don't fear them...'

'For sure!'

The American tells me his name - Karim - and I immediately recognise the sound as being remarkably similar to one of the *bij mantras*, sometimes intoned silently for meditation practice.

'Sounds like your *mantra*,' I declare impulsively.

'Thank you,' he says seriously.

As I walk on, an idea slowly comes to mind. Though I had long since come to a decision to avoid smoking cannabis, I scan the hedges to see if I can spot any marijuana plants growing. No sooner do I start to look for them than I am overtaken by a young Indian who turns to me and asks: -

'You want to smoke? Here, I have *charas*,' he says holding out a lump of hashish.

Now, I ask myself, how come he suddenly offered me the hash now, just after I had that thought, when usually I am not being offered it?

'No, thank you,' I hear myself reply.

'You want? You want?' he asks again.

I shake my head; the desire has come and gone almost in an instant.

'My name Sagori is.'

'*Dhanyavad,*' I say, thanking him.

* * *

Later in the day, back at the hotel, Susan and I meet and decide to join up for a walk together. I discover her to be not only a seasoned hiker but also profoundly interested in nature.

'Do you know the name of that flower there,' I ask, referring to a flowering shrub that grows locally here in great abundance.

'In South Africa they call it *Lanten*.' She answers, 'It's a real nuisance.'

'Are you sure it's the same? It has such beautifully scented delicate blossoms, sometimes pink, sometimes orange.'

'I'm sure of it! It's a pest, in much the same way as Japanese Knotweed is in England. As it happens it was an English woman who introduced *Lanten* into India, way back in the days of Colonial rule. Just one cutting, now it's everywhere.'

Finding that Susan intends staying in the area only a few days, and realising she is so obviously the outdoor type, I mention the white-water rafting activities upstream on the Ganga. She seems interested, very interested. I also suggest that she might take a trip higher into the hills, to gain a sight of the snow-clad mountains on the Tibetan border. The idea appeals to her greatly and as we discuss her options a thought occurs to me - the Hindi books I am looking for are probably still available from the monastery at Joshimath.

'I've been thinking of taking a break from here and perhaps travelling into the hills,' I announce.

'So we could travel together?'

'Sure. I'm trying to find some books. Some years ago they were on sale at the monastery in Joshimath. They was there when I visited before.'

'But, only if you want to go,' she says, 'I don't want you to come on my account.'

'I'll give it some thought.'

As we continue strolling, I detail for her the byways and paths through the dense forest of *Sal* trees we are walking. Many unusual shrubs and trees grow here, such as *Euphorbia* and the ash-like Ailanthus 'tree of heaven'.

Eventually our walk brings us to the base of a hill.

'I would take you up to the *ashram* there but I no longer have any attachment to it,' I comment.

Almost as soon as the words leave my lips a group of people suddenly become visible a little way ahead, having turned a bend in the path. Behind them walks an ochre-robed *swami*, lean and tall, with his hair tied atop of his head in a topknot. In his arms he carries a long object enclosed within an orange cloth bag clutched against his chest. This I assume is a wooden *danda*, a staff. I pay him attention purely on the basis of his being a *dandi* or stick-carrying *swami*, since they are rare even amongst holy men.

One brief look at his radiant face is enough to convince that this *dandi swami* is definitely a high soul, his eyes reveal deep jewelled pools of light that twinkle and dance. In fact his face immediately reminds me of another's, now seen only in the photographs and paintings; the face of a former Shankaracharya of Jyotir Math who passed away almost fifty years before, whose books I am searching...

I fairly fly into the *dandi swami's* face, gaining his attention.

He appears very pleased as I invoke the name of the departed Shankaracharya and he rolls his head gently, his eyes sparkling even more than before. With a graceful gesture of the wrist he gently communicates his desire for me to walk with him. I follow him and am surprised that only with great effort is it possible to keep pace. The path we take leads us up the side of the hill, up past the many uninhabited beehive-like stone buildings there. At length, at the top of the path, the *swami* turns to the right and stops at one of the beehive dwellings, where he slips off his sandals, unlocks the door and ushers me forward to go within.

Once inside the small building he points to a framed photograph placed centrally on a table. It is a rare and beautifully presented photograph of Shankaracharya Swami Brahmananda Saraswati - 'Guru Dev' - who died back in 1953, but whose name has continued to be respected ever since. Reverently, with hands placed together, I gaze at the portrait.

In truth I am stunned that fate should deliver me this opportunity of meeting one of the few living disciples of the holyman in the photograph. I now study the other two framed photographs set upon the table; and note that one of them is of the Shankaracharya's successor, Swami Shantanand Saraswati.

The other picture is of an old man that I cannot identify. As I stand musing I am suddenly aware of that the old *swami* is again standing beside me. He chuckles merrily and points first at himself and then at the photo. But I am thrown into confusion for the picture appears to be of a much older man and I puzzle as to how the *swami* could look so much fresher and younger now than when the photograph had been taken?

Then I suddenly remember Susan, and it occurs to me that I should go and find out whether or not she has followed us, so I turn to go outside. Coincidentally, Susan is just now arriving, and I can tell from her expression that she is unsure how to conduct herself in the company of this aged monk.

'It is the custom to take off one's shoes, as a sign of respect,' I offer. Obligingly she begins to unlace her boots, but the *swami* interrupts and beckons her to go in and look at the photographs. She has had insufficient time to unlace her boots and so I fret that the *swami* will take offence at her oversight. And I wait for the roar! But I worry needlessly, for he appears blissfully unconcerned about her footwear.

So I relax and look about me, and observe that nailed above the doorway hangs a hand-painted strip of metal, which states in Devanagari script the *swami's* name; that of 'Dandi Swami Narayananand Saraswati'.

When Susan rejoins me outside and I whisper to her: -

'I believe he has achieved the goal of his *sadhana*, his path of spiritual practice. He seems to me to be totally at peace, in want of nothing.'

She confides that she has no previous experience whatever of meetings with Indian holymen, which to me makes her sound as though she is doubtful about what I'm saying to her.

'It is customary to leave a gift,' I whisper. 'Have you any fruit or biscuits perhaps?'

'No, sorry!'

'Some small offering, we could leave those blossoms you're holding.'

'Yes, fine.'

Swami Ji settles down to sit on the wooden table outside his dwelling. He makes himself comfortable and by gestures, facial expressions and endearing chuckles the *swami* puts us at our ease. He takes a piece of white chalk and writes a word in Hindi on a chalkboard -

मौन

- '*maun*' (a vow of silence). This explains the lack of conversation, but he appears happy enough to write simple answers to my few questions.

I mention Jyotir Math (the monastery of the Northern Shankaracharya) and I can't help remarking to Susan: -

'It seems as though this meeting is a message for us to travel to the mountains and go to Joshimath.' I laugh, and Susan grins her agreement.

Again, involuntarily, I find myself sobbing gently and am again incapable of speaking much before more tears well up. I feel compelled to explain to the *swami* that since visiting a poor man locally I have been taken with this condition, for some days. Swami Ji begins to write on the chalkboard again and I puzzle the meaning of the what he is writing, spelling out two unfamiliar words;

वेरी गूद

'W-E-R-E-E G-U-U-D'.

At first I don't get the meaning, and then I hear the sound of the words in my head. Shaking with mirth as I interpret their meaning.

'VERY GOOD?' I ask. 'Really? Good, good! Thank you Swami Ji.'

For several minutes I bask in the lightness and good humour of this saintly man. Then, when I sense I should take my leave, I feel a strong compulsion to signal my very great respect for the *swami*. I find myself not only lowering my head, but suddenly and quite involuntarily throwing myself onto the dusty ground with my arms outstretched to touch his feet. Then I feel his hands hover behind my head as if in blessing.

Positively glowing, I now accompany Susan away from the *swami*'s presence.

'I've never thrown myself at the feet of anyone in my life!' I confide to her, 'But then I've never met such a man before. We have been blessed indeed. Did you notice how when he moves it is so graceful, as if there were not a bone in his body?'

Susan smiles.

'As we are up here, would you like to take a walk about the *ashram*?' I suggest to Susan, pointing to a grove of palm trees.

A man's voice calls out, from out of nowhere: -

'No, no, you should not go.'

We walk on, only to find our way obstructed.

'It soon dark is,' the man informs us. 'Tomorrow you are coming. Yes, tomorrow come again.'

So, Susan and I retrace our steps downhill and after just a few minutes we notice that the sun is already disappearing from view, leaving washes of red streaks in the bright blue evening sky. In the short time it takes to re-join the main concrete path into the village darkness descends, very rapidly.

'He was right, you know, we would have been wandering around up there in the dark.'

Entering the village, the glittering bright lights of the shops offer a dazzling spectacle. The pretty lights reflect and sparkle on the many colourful goods displayed there.

Susan marvels at the sight, as do I, for it is as if everything has been brushed by magic. The sounds enchant too, and the air hangs with sweet pungent aromas, there is the smell of incense mixed with the smell of fresh citrus fruits. I am minded that the name 'Swargashram' means '*ashram* of Heaven' or '*ashram* of Paradise' and I imagine that a marketplace in paradise could hold no greater feast for the senses.

All-at-once both Susan and myself hear the sound of beautiful music floating up from the riverside. As we go to investigate we find there a swathe of pilgrims celebrating evening prayers accompanied by some very fine musicians, with the sounds of voices and instruments being routed through a powerful public address system. As I survery the amassed crowds I notice a concentration of dozens of spluttering orange flames emanating from a brass holder which is carried and passed over the heads of the swaying singing congregation gathered, who stand packed tightly together on the steps leading down to the Ganga. And there, amidst the rushing waters, is a massive statue of Lord Shiva, which sits facing us all. From all directions come flashes of light, as multiple cameras capture these magic moments.

*

On the way back at Hotel Rajdeep I meet a neighbour to whom I tell about the celebrations. 'There is a huge event next to Parmarth Niketan Ashram - quite unbelievable,' I rave.

'Oh yes. They do it every night, it's Aarti,' she explains, somewhat flatly.

'Are you sure? I think it must have been particularly special tonight. There were people videoing it. And the sound system… it was just amazing, like some free concert. The musicians must have been professionals, they were brilliant!'

She looks at me doubtfully as if I am exaggerating. I change the subject.

I recall I had chanced on her along with others earlier, who were going off to a party, a fancy dress affair, and this particular young lady had woven the stalks and fruits of limes into her hair, presenting herself as an advanced *yoga asana* in which 'ones sexual energy is sublimated to become spiritual energy'. Accompanying her that night was the bearded French meteorologist decked out as an Indian woman in a *sari*. Actually, in an odd sort of way, it suited him.

'How was the Halloween party then?' I ask.

'Oh, you should have come, you would have enjoyed it.'

'It looks like I'm off to the mountains!' I announce. 'I've been thinking of going up there for a while now, and today I met with a *sannyasi* associated with the monastery in Joshimath. It seems like a message. I think I've got to go.'

She looks at me.

'But perhaps Joshimath has come to you?' she suggests thoughtfully.

Chapter Six

'*Namaste* Chaturvedi Ji,' I greet the hotel manager with my hands placed together.

'*Namaste* to you Sir, and how you are sleeping?'

'Actually, I awoke to find the balcony door open.'

'That is okay. It is safe; no one will come in room. You are worried?'

I have no wish to conceal my concern over the lapse of attentiveness which left me vulnerable to theft, I merely smile weakly, still puzzled how I came to fall asleep on the bed and spend the coldest hours of the night uncovered. The truth is that, since my arrival in Rishikesh, I have felt no great urge to sleep, so I tend to read, listen to tapes, or just lie thinking until the early hours, sleeping for no more than three hours. I most often arise about five in the morning, which is a novelty in itself, and have more than enough time to meditate, tidy and clean before starting the day.

'Can I order breakfast? Oh and can I pay yesterday's bills too?' I ask.

'*Conflax*, milk, *jamtost* and big tea?'

'Plain toast today please.'

'No *conflax* you want?' he queries, wrinkling his brow.

'Yes, cornflakes I want and toast and tea,' I answer in Pidgin English. In fact, what with trying to speak the local tongue, my grasp of English seems to be slipping fast.

'Hot milk or cold milk, Sir?' Chaturvedi asks.

'Very hot please,' I reply emphatically, believing that boiled milk is more likely to be free from harmful bacteria.

Mercifully, eating out in these parts is fairly trouble free and there are many restaurants and cafes to choose from, all of them vegetarian. And most places serve excellent North Indian dishes including *thali* (an all-in-one meal consisting of various dishes; vegetables, pulses, rice and Indian breads such as *puri* or *roti*). Some restaurants also include a fair selection of western foods on their menus, such as the Choti Wala which is a firm favourite with many visitors. Choti Wala is advertised as 'India Fame Restaurant - Homely Delicious Meals & Snacks' and it boasts a roof-top dining area overlooking the bustling main walkway where hawkers tote their wares, such as toys and slide whistles, whilst others offer to print one's hands and arms with designs applied by hennaed wooden blocks. Soliciting for business outside the restaurant sits a bizarre looking man coloured with pink body paint; he is the 'Choti Wala' whose hair is shaven off save for a lone tuft of long hair (*choti*) which is waxed to a point atop of his bald head.

There are also some other particularly good places to eat across the river, near to the ferry crossing point, notably the East-West, with it's excellent Italian dishes and the Shanti Café, which, on occasion, even offers home-made apple pie and yoghurt ice cream! Here it is that I meet with a shaven headed *yoga* exponent, wearing a bright orange Omkarananda Ashram T-shirt. Confidently he gives out details of his weekly agenda to two Japanese students who are seemingly attentive to his every word. The cafe is small and his voice is very audible.

'So this is what I will be doing with my week, that is, unless anything unexpected occurs!' he announces rather self-importantly.

I reflect that virtually all my meetings of late have been unforeseen. This meeting too, and as our eyes meet I hear my voice call across to him, clearly and firmly: -

'Everything is unexpected my friend...! Everything!'

He gapes at me, surprised.

'Yes, yes of course,' he answers uncertainly. Uncharacteristically for me, I make no attempt to explain myself, but instead get up to leave.

I make my way back across the river by the Ram Jhula Bridge, pausing only to buy a few *rupees* worth of doughballs to feed the fishes, after which I set off on a long circular walk via Lakshman Jhula and on the return journey I take the hill road.

The desire to get back to nature reasserts itself again, so I take a solitary wander in the leafy wilds and pursue the course of a rushing stream. Soon I begin to hear the faint sound of tumbling gushing water and am thrilled to realise I am near to a waterfall. As the sound becomes louder I notice my surroundings becoming increasingly scenic and marvel at the flowering boughs that overhang the path, the blooms and blossoms of the pink and purple flowers that have fallen to form a rich carpet over the smooth mossy rocks on which I walk. It is as if I have found the resting-place of a local god. I proceed cautiously but find myself to be totally alone. Sitting down close to the waterfall I again feel the deep, deep peace

I recently felt in the presence of the *dandi swami*. I breathe deeply filling myself full with the peace and freshness of this sacred spot.

Leaving the waterfall, I descend again and somewhat lower downstream I find some villagers washing their clothes in the swirling waters, beating the garments against one of the many large rocks strewn about the stream. I guess people have been doing their laundry like this since time immemorial.

I continue descending the hill, and the path I take brings me to a pleasant shaded glade where I pause to rest. Then, all at once, the sounds of leaves rustling and twigs moving alert me to the presence of company, whereupon I see a full size *langur* urgently moving towards me. I remain there standing quite still. The *langur* comes close, standing to his full height, and moves to within a couple of feet from me. Barring his crooked teeth he begins to gibber, to grind his teeth and to hiss loudly. I stare with interest at his almost human hands, with their refined fingers and nails, and study too his long powerful feet which resemble those of a wolf, and I marvel at his astonishingly long tale tail which sweeps the ground. The *langur* monkey continues to chatter and gesture excitedly at me. At length, in order to avoid unnecessary exposure to any further danger, I feel moved to wander slowly away.

A little later, telling my story to a local, he smiles as he explains: '*Langur* want for food!'

'Really?' I ask doubtfully.

'Yes, possible to bring fruit for *langur*? You can feed. Just hold out hand and him will take.'

Though most *langur* seem gentle enough, I have yet to see anyone go very close to them, let alone feed them. It must be said, that a wild animal can do a lot of damage to exposed human flesh and since I am stripped to the waist I am in no mind to place myself in a position where I might get mauled.

*

Rather than use a laundry service, many travellers prefer to clean their own clothes, as evidenced by the improvised washing lines strung across most of the hotel balconies. After spot cleaning with a bar of soap and then soaking my clothes in a bucket of water and washing powder, I rinse my garments out and watch as they drip, drip-dry in the hot breeze, satisfied that they will be ready before the afternoon is done. I then begin sorting some photographs recently collected from the mini-lab in Rishikesh market, carefully sequencing the snaps before slipping them into the complimentary albums thoughtfully provided. But as I busy myself, I am all too aware of the fact that I have several unresolved issues on my mind. Amongst my concerns is the ongoing question of whether or not to embark on the course in Reiki. I reason that since I have never envisaged myself as a 'healer' it is fairly pointless to embark on a training course in the art of healing. Having swiftly dealt with this problem I feel more than confident to deal with the much easier task of deciding whether or not to travel to the mountains. But, despite my initial confidence, I find it difficult to come to a decision, even after concentratedly and repeatedly assessing the pros and cons.

Unexpectedly, whilst I am thinking about travel ideas, Susan pops by my room to announce she is planning to move on to Mussoorie, a hill station some fifty miles northwest of Rishikesh. Though she makes it clear she is still open to the idea of taking a bus into the hills we agree to postpone further discussion until we have better information on how long the return journey might take.

So, with that settled I spend my time on whatever comes to mind, listening to music, reading a little, and dealing with my laundry.

Nirmoha drops in to see me later.

Usually I welcome the chance to get better acquainted, to trade philosophies, discuss points of view and enjoy a glass of strong *chaay* with her, but on this occasion, I am slightly ill at ease as I am mindful of my resolve to turn down the offer of the Reiki instruction. Something stops me announcing my decision; so it seems that my mind is not as firmly made up as I thought. Reiki sounds harmless enough and might even prove to have something to offer, but I have to deal with the possibility that Nirmoha might wish me to become her pupil rather than simply share her knowledge with me. I take the opportunity of her visit to voice this concern. I am very surprised to find that she offers no reassurance whatsoever, quite the opposite in fact.

'I only take beginners!' she says seriously. 'You will be learning Level One Reiki. It takes the completion of Levels One, Two and Three to become a qualified Reiki Master.'

Actually, I rather suspect that this Reiki teaching might be a back-door entry into the world of the 'Orange People', the followers of Rajneesh who are notorious for their permissive attitude towards sex. I am open to other paths but I don't want to be drawn unwittingly into a cult.

'What sort of meditation do you teach, if any, on the Reiki course?' I ask. 'I mean... well... well you have a photo of Osho in your room and er.. Well I wondered..?'

She laughs as she divines the meaning behind my question.

'Oh I don't teach Dynamic Meditation,' she answers brightly, referring to the five-stage practice of: -

1. Rapid deep breathing.

2. Catharthis e.g. laughing, shouting, screaming jumping and shaking.

3. Jumping on the balls of the feet whilst repeating the sound 'Hoo-Hoo-Hoo'.

4. Remaining motionless.

5. Dancing.

Nirmoha offers no further clarification on what techniques she imparts and, as I have been advised by her not to read any books on Reiki prior to instruction, it seems I am expected to make a total leap of faith!

*

Rameshwar Das

After my recent chance meetings with Rameshwar Das and the blissful *swami* in the jungle I find I have a need to clarify to myself what I have learned, if anything, from the meetings. I ponder but without reaching any conclusions. In truth I find that sometimes it is good to set one's thoughts down, since it often helps make better sense of them (my pocketbook is used for jotting down reminders, shopping lists, addresses and phone numbers, and contains many notes addressed to myself).

Putting pen to paper I begin to weigh my thoughts about the *dandi swami*:

> *'He doesn't have anything I do not,*
>
> *but he has far far more of it,*
>
> *and more importantly,*
>
> *he can cope with that moreness,*
>
> *more simple now.'*

Clearly, the state of blissful grace he enjoys must be as the result of patient work. But, I ask myself, has he gained something he once lacked or has he rediscovered something that was formerly hidden? More than likely, in his devotions, he has discovered ways to slough off those impediments that block the smooth operation of his sensory functions.

I wonder if all of us were to perceive fear, ignorance and unwelcome stress, as our enemies, and then take every available means to rid our minds and bodies of their influence, perhaps we too could witness the truth of his master's teaching: -

'The dawn comes to dispel the darkness of night, allowing us to enjoy the light of the sun (which is self-illuminating). Spiritual teachings destroy ignorance and therefore remove darkness, but they cannot throw light on the inner Self, for the Self is Light.'

- Swami Brahmananda Saraswati

Chapter Seven

'Wait a moment,' Susan shouts out, somewhat flustered to the rapping at her door.

'It's only me!' I assure her, 'If it's not convenient, I can come back later.'

'Just hang on a minute...! Is that okay?'

'Fine, no problem, take your time.'

It is not long before I hear the sound of a bolt being released followed by the creak of the opening door, which seemingly signals that I am free to enter. So, cautiously, I poke my head through the gap.

'Yes, do come on in,' she invites, moving briskly back into the room, and winding a towel around her dripping hair. Barelegged and draped only in a loose blouse of turquoise satin tastefully printed with dragon designs, she hovers about self-consciously until deciding to shuffle and slide into her four-season sleeping bag. Then, leaning over to one side she draws closer to herself a pile of papers, apparently they are uncompleted art works.

'You don't mind if I carry on with these do you? We can still talk.'

She sets to work on one of an assortment of designs, and with deft confident strokes she begins pulling the pastels this way and that, sideways over the paper, producing sensuous shifts of abstract shapes. As she works, Susan speaks of her travel plans within India and how she intends to then fly on to Bangkok before eventually returning to England. When the conversation lapses, I wonder whether to broach a subject which I have been giving a good deal of consideration.

'I've been thinking about maybe teaching meditation,' I remark rather hesitantly.

'Good idea,' Susan responds enthusiastically.

'It's just.. it's just that there is nobody that teaches meditation where I live, so I figure that maybe I should start.'

'You should!'

'Well, the idea came to me during my evening meditation. You're the first person I have told.'

'Thank you.'

'But does it make any sense to you that I feel I need to give myself permission?'

'Completely. But you're so obviously sincere about your beliefs and you've spent so much time finding out about all these things. So tell me, how will you advertise?'

'Advertise? Well I certainly wouldn't charge anything.'

'Great. But you've got to let people know. Perhaps you could put up cards.'

'Something like "Blessings from the Himalayas, at no cost"?'

'Great,' she enthuses.

'Well, thanks for the encouragement,' I say, rising to leave, 'Oh, by the way, have you had any more thoughts about our trip into the hills?'

She furrows her brow.

'From what I can gather it is rather a long way', she says, 'someone said it would take two days to get to Joshimath. Is that right?'

'Mmmm. I think maybe that it is. Possibly stop a night in Srinagar and make it there the next day,' I suggest, rather sheepishly. 'Then a couple of nights at least in Joshimath else it's not really worth while going.'

'A week! What's it like up there, is it very beautiful?'

'Well it's very high up, you're really close to the high mountains and it's a good spot for hiking but I'm not going to try and sell the idea to you. It is a long way and basically I'm really going there for two books!

'Well I'm planning to go to Mussoorie in a few days.'

'So perhaps we should forget about the trip, it was a good idea but..'

'But.. it's going to take too long... ' she admits.

'So, it looks like we're not going to go after all. I think we would have been good company, but the more I think about the long bus trip..'

'Yes, I agree, but thanks for the offer anyway. It was a really nice idea.'

'I'll leave you to get on now, thanks for the chat, I really appreciate it,' I thank her warmly.

Talking with Susan has brought me reassurance and considerable support for my intention to share the knowledge of simple meditation. However, what I haven't mentioned to her is that, at the moment I came to this decision, it was during meditation, and an image of Shankaracharya

Swami Brahmananda flashed into my mind. He appeared facing me and seemed to bow his head slightly as if in approval. Though I wonder whether my imagination could have generated this 'vision', I feel blessed anyway.

I recall that as I enjoyed the image of this venerable teacher coming to my mind, two Sanskrit words sprang to my awareness. I wonder, could my mind have created these too? And more importantly, what exactly do the words mean?

On my way back to my own room I have to cross the hotel lobby and whilst there I stop and talk with Chaturvedi Ji.

'I have been thinking of going to Joshimath but it is too much far. I am needing to get some books there for a friend. By phone it is possible to contact the monastery?'

'Joshimath. I will see if someone is going that way. But why you not get in marketplace?' he suggests innocently.

'These are rare books, they are very much difficult to find, but maybe.. With your help?'

'You have titles?'

'Oh yes.'

'You write them down and I am asking for you from friend in Swargashram bookshop.'

'That's a brilliant idea. Thanks a lot.'

'It is pleasure. We do what we can for to making you enjoy your stay. You are leaving it with me and I do my best for you,' he says pocketing the book list I have written. He crosses his arms.. 'Leave it to me, I make necessary inquiries.'

*

A fellow guest, Alok, a longhaired Indian lad from Kashmir has kitted himself out with the unlikely name of 'Mr Ali'.

'Where I live there are many Muslims,' he explains. 'I don't like problems,' he adds, adjusting his sunglasses and lighting a cigarette.

'But you still follow Hindu beliefs,' I ask him.

'Of course! Ah, I see you have sacred thread bracelet,' he observes. Seemingly he is favourably impressed.

'It was on a visit to Neelkanth Mahadev, there is a white temple up above

Neelkanth where I received *prasad*, a flower and the thread.

'Neelkanth Mahadev is Lord Shiva,' Alok states, and from his wallet he plucks something out and passes it to me. It is a silvery holographic picture of the god Shiva seated in meditation wearing snakes about his neck and arms. The image of a trident flashes before him, glowing in spectral colours.

'This is for you Paul.'

'Oh! It is very, very beautiful. I will treasure it.'

Mr. Ali smiles.

*

Walking along a corridor in Hotel Rajdeep I encounter Nirmoha again.

'How would you like a Reiki session this morning?' Nirmoha asks me.

Her offer comes as a complete surprise, for as I understand it, this is the first day for a long time that she has been free from teaching.

'Are you sure?' I puzzle, 'But yesterday, you said you were taking the day off. You wanted to go to Hardwar.'

'I thought it would be better to give you Reiki, that is, if you're interested?'

How can I refuse? This seems like the perfect opportunity to discover the mysteries of Reiki, as a recipient rather than a pupil, and I am not about to pass it up.

'Where? When?' I ask.

It seems I have time to take a shower, and on Nirmoha's advice, I change into looser clothing.

At the appointed time, I make my way to the end of the corridor and find the door to the last room is open. The smell of incense hangs in the air. I slip off my flip-flops and enter. The room is noticeably uncluttered, tidy and very clean. I note that a mattress, wrapped in a white sheet, has been placed in the middle of the floor.

Nirmoha instructs me to lie down on the mattress; arms by my sides, legs placed together and eyes closed. In soothing tones she gives further instruction, first for me to relax, then to let the mattress take my weight, and then, to let go …..

Having 'let go' I am now guided to place my attention on the music which is playing softly in the background. It becomes a pleasant form of meditation and I soon find myself completely released from all concerns. Only very, very gradually do I sense the presence of hands hovering near my head. Slowly head and hands merge. Within myself I am aware of a sudden increase in light - my senses have become heightened, I notice the notes of music now sound clearer, somehow more natural, as though they were not produced on instruments but by nature itself. Witnessing the sounds, and the scents in the air. and my own thoughts, I gradually become removed from identification with my body and my mind.

I suddenly sense what feels like droplets of liquid being placed around my eyes. I feel similar sensations repeated elsewhere across my body. Very slowly a realisation crystallises, that precious stones are being placed upon me. As I lie here absorbing these new sensations and enjoying them, I sense warmth about my eyes which now increases, as though a dormant energy in the precious stones has become awakened and is springing into life.

I witness as tears begin to flow from my eyes, trickling down my cheeks. Spasms of energy ripple through me, manifesting as sudden jerks of my neck. I can hear myself let out gentle sighs. As the warm hands touch or hover elsewhere, similar twitches, sighs and jerkings ensue.

I become aware of my breathing and notice that at times it is only barely perceptible, and then suddenly the breathing becomes rapid, but just as quickly it subsides. All the time I am a witness, as if the events are not really connected to the inner watching me. A sudden brief sadness visits me, and I sense the gemstones have been removed; and then I hear the sounds of sighs coming from my mouth. Only very gradually does the body stop twitching. I lie and listen to sounds surfacing through the quiet; it is then that I notice that the music is no longer playing.

At length I hear a voice, the voice is very faint, and it is some time before the message of the voice connects with my thinking mind and finds a response. The voice requests me to slowly open my eyes and sit up. I find my eyes opening and am surprised and pleased to see Nirmoha sitting nearby.

'Perhaps you should go back to your room now and lie down quietly for some few minutes,' she advises me.

Obediently I arise but only slowly.

In a state of wonder I make the distance back to my room and lie down on my bed, and am fascinated by the involuntary twists and turns my body takes as it attempts to rest. The movements gradually subside and I become still, as eventually I resume identification with my body. Having still no desire to move, I remain for far longer than the few minutes recommended.

A sound in the room alerts me to the fact I am not alone, the voice asks me to open my eyes.

'Are you okay?' Nirmoha asks, sounding concerned.

'Fine, fine, fine,' I answer, sitting up gradually, looking about me in wonder and bewilderment. A stream of sunshine floods the room.

'How do you fancy taking lunch at Shanti?' Nirmoha asks.

'That was really amazing what happened there, but I'm fine, in fact I'm really, really hungry.'

I am suddenly aware that again I have full use of my body and mind and I have a wish to make the very most of the day.

Nirmoha's concerned expression melts into a grin of satisfaction. I surmise that she is relieved to see I have emerged, fresh and rejuvenated, as I suspect that she was taken by surprise at the apparent intensity of my experiences at her hands.

Chapter Eight

'Love all. Share what you have with all. Give, give, give. Become rich at heart by giving all that you have. Expand your heart. This is the key to Cosmic Consciousness.'

- Swami Shivanand

Becoming a *sannyasi* in his late thirties, Swami Shivanand Saraswati settled in Rishikesh, founded Shivanand Ashram and formed the Divine Life Society. Before leaving his body in 1963, at the age of 75 years old, he created no less than 300 volumes of spiritual literature.

Whilst I'm walking about the village or the jungle, I sometimes meet with a monk called Swami Radhakrishnanand, a committed Indian devotee of Shivanand, and on each occasion he presents me with a copy of the *ashram* magazine *'The Divine Life'*. A voracious reader himself, this *swami* encourages me to study the teachings of his master, and to this end he selectively underlines a selection of publications from the *ashram* booklist for my attention. Such titles such as *'All about Hinduism'*, *'Bliss Divine'*, *'Hindu Fasts and Festivals'*, *'Inspiring Songs and Kirtans'*, *'Inspiring Stories'*, *'Lives of Saints'*, *'Lord Shiva and His Worship'* and *'What Becomes of the Soul After Death'*. It is this monk's way of trying to involve me in his beliefs, however, as I explain, I am already acquainted with Swami Shivanand's teachings.

'I have visited the room in the *ashram* where Swami Shivanand did his writing,' I tell him, 'It still has all his belongings in it, like his nail clippers, his pen and blanket...'

'Yes!'

'There is a good feel about the place.'

'You should come to lecture at *ashram*! You wish?'

'Thank you. Maybe I will.'

'You come!'

'Do you know Dandi Swami Narayananand?' I enquire.

'Yes I know him. He lives without clothes.'

'Mmm. I think you mean a different *swami*.'

'No, Dandi Swami, he speaks at *ashram*.'

'Really. When I met with him he was in *maun*, he was not speaking.'

'You want? You can get recordings of him? Yes, you can get at 'Swar Sangam' music shop; they sell cassettes of Swami Ji. Or you can get at Parmarth Niketan.'

I am intrigued at the prospect of hearing the voice of the silent *dandi swami*. In point of fact I become instantly attached to the task of tracking down these recordings and start to nurture a desire to be present at one of the talks.

'Thanks a lot,' I say springing to my feet, 'I think I will go to find cassettes right now! *Namaste Ji*'

'*Namaste Ji*, you come to *ashram* for lecture?'

'We shall see. We don't plan,' I answer evasively.

*

'Dandi Swami? Yes I am knowing him,' the local record shop owner informs me, 'Dandi Swami he is speaking at Parmarth Niketan Ashram every time evening. It is possible I can get tape recordings of him.'

'This *swami*, his name is Narayananand, he is staying at Shankaracharya Nagar?' I tell him.

'Yes, yes I know him. I get you recording? Yes? Or you go Parmarth Niketan? These recordings also they are having there.'

'Sure?'

'Yes, I am sure you can get. No problem.'

So, I walk along the riverfront to pay a visit to the glorious buildings of Parmarth Niketan but the lady secretary there initially meets my questions guardedly, with a blank look.

'But I am told Swami Ji speaks here!' I continue.

'Yes,' she admits frostily.

'So. Can I get recording of him?'

'He Sanskrit is speaking.'

'But, I can obtain recording?'

'Yes.'

'You have cassettes then?'

'No.'

'Where can I get them?'

'You must bring machine. Seven in evening come,' she says, seemingly warming, but only very slightly.

I find the woman's manner off-putting but the opportunity to see and hear the *dandi swami* speak is altogether too important to pass up on account of a conflict of personalities. So, I return early in the evening and on this occasion I come tape recorder in hand.

I arrive early, with enough time to catch a few minutes of the *Aarti* celebration on the waterfront. After leaving my socks and shoes at the gate, I find a good spot to watch and record the ceremony, which even now is already in full swing. There are musicians playing and are accompanied by the yellow-clad choristers who are singing the evening prayers, joined by the swaying crowds who fervently sing along. Clusters of flickering flames atop of brass stands are passed aloft and over the gathered congregation.

By seven o'clock the ceremony is over, and the crowd begins to disperse whereupon I return to Parmarth Niketan but I find no *dandi swami* there, instead I am directed to try elsewhere, at a site upstream past Ram Jhula Bridge.

I scour the area along the shore, investigating all the wayside buildings, but still gain no sight of him. Before giving up I make one last ditch bid at finding him, and enter a simple *ashram* where an old monk is addressing a congregation of Indians, women on the left, men on the right. I wait there, hoping to speak with someone.

I catch sight of his staff and pennant close by to him. And I start to wonder if I have actually found the *dandi swami,* but I do not recognise him at all. It is just a feeling but he seems to be a very sincere man. So I sit down as unobtrusively as is possible and I listen as he leads the congregation into prayers and then he lectures them. Though appearing subdued and serious he nonetheless delivers his message with the unwavering conviction expected of a qualified *guru*. I gaze at the face of the speaker, but without recognition, noting his cropped grey hair, his stubble beard and his very serious expression. I study the painting behind him, a sideview portrait of an elderly man, apparently naked, presumably his teacher.

After battling with the disappointment that the monk's presence has provoked no wave of recognition, joy or inspiration in me, I make a move to leave the gathering, pausing only briefly to read a notice fixed outside the *ashram*.

I make my way back to the village where I am instantly spotted by friend Sanjay, the record store owner.

'You are finding Dandi Swami?'

'I no longer require the tape.'

'You don't like recording?' he asks frowning.

'I have made recording, but I discovered that your *dandi swami's* name is Hansanand, a very different *swami* from the one I met with the other day.'

What I do not mention is that after making two fruitless trips to Parmarth Niketan and one to Hansanand's *ashram*, I am becoming increasingly frustrated with the inaccuracy of information I am getting. However, I suspect these experiences will only strengthen my resolve to forthwith focus less attention on tape recordings and more on maintaining my composure of mind!

*

When I next speak with Susan she tells me she will soon be leaving Rishikesh and I make a mental note to try to meet up with her to say a proper goodbye before she leaves. It occurs to me to ask whether or not she can remember what the *swami* we met looks like.

'I can remember him very well!' she says very self-assuredly.

'Brilliant! I can't explain why, but I cannot visualise him at all.' So I ask Susan; 'I wonder if you could do a sketch of him for me?'

'Sure,' she answers immediately.

But suddenly frowning, Susan adds slowly, 'I would need him to be there for me to be able to do the drawing.'

It seems that she has suddenly become aware that her own memory might fail her also.

'Ha!' I exclaim. 'That rather defeats the purpose doesn't it? Well no matter. It rather looks as though I must pay Dandi Swami another visit then!'

*

The following day, when I sit to meditate I am surprised to find that I feel unusually relaxed and calm, and as I begin my practice I discover I am unable to do other than witness the most glorious feeling of happiness - my senses fill with fresh bright light. I cannot detect any rise and fall of my breath; it is clear I am not breathing at all, though my senses are fully sharpened and alert. My mind is almost inactive, seldom does a thought arise; it is only with effort that I manage to sustain a thought for more than a few moments before it dissolves back into formlessness and a super intense light.

There is still no breath, and then there stirs a faint sigh of air and then again there is no breath.

Smiling deeply I try again to compose my thinking, only to find that I can only sustain a flow of thought for a few seconds, before again and again I merge back into a steady, knowing, loving light - plunging into a vast full pool of euphoria.

At length, the impulse to open my eyes arises. I sit there glowing with happiness, whilst chuckling softly. Eventually my reverie is overtaken by a thought - the thought to get up and take this wonderfully clear energy out into the world beyond my room.

It appears that the real purpose of meditation, whilst seated comfortably with the eyes closed, is to attain a blissful state of no-thought.

Whilst such periods of no-thought are being experienced the mind becomes very satisfied and when the meditation is over, and one gets on with one's daily existence, the benefit of this brush with superconsciousness lingers and gives one a big lift.

I feel so very deeply relaxed, and spectacularly energised, so accordingly, having no wish to delay in getting out and about, I get myself ready to go out. After locking my room I scoot along the landing, bounce downstairs and through to the lobby where I happen upon Susan who is just now checking out of the hotel. The amiable hotel manager watches us with apparent curiosity as we hug and well-wish (it is of note that Indians generally do not seem to indulge in such public displays of affection).

After Susan's departure Chaturvedi Ji calls me over.

'You now are going for more walking?'

'Yes, I am off to visit the *swami* I met with the other day.'

Chaturvedi Ji looks at me intently.

'If you have some minutes before you go out... I should like to tell you some things of this my life. It could take some long time, but if you have patience for me...?'

I nod.

'You know I have not always worked at this hotel?'

'Sure.'

'You see, my wife is dying seventeen years before. Until then I am working Reliance Petro-Chemical and Cloth. I left employ at fifty-two years of age and I am giving most money to daughter to look after remaining son at home. Everywhere I am travelling in India before I am meeting with my *sadhu* in the forest. No speech he made, only he gave me food, and in the night, which was very cold, he came with blanket to keep me warm. Eventually, it was time to move on and then he spoke only to tell me 'You will come again'.

'I continue travelling about India for quite some time and then arrived in Prayag where I met with very rich lady who took me home. Her husband is millionaire. Anyway this lady and myself we have argument, for I think she is too much identified with wealth and beauty and she feels superior to me. So I leave that place, but before I go she is telling to me that a feeling of love has been growing in her for me. But still I went, anyway.

'Then, after some time, I must return to Prayag, I did not want to go but I am to attend a wedding there. I am very uneasy in my mind, so again I leave Prayag. But I did again return and then I visit her. She showed me letter she has just this day written to me - there was no trace of anger or problem coming from her side. It was as nothing was not good between us.

'Soon after again meeting with this lady I am hearing that my son has been injured in United States in hang gliding accident. She immediately went to U.S. for fifteen months and paid all money for him. Everything for hospital, for food, for everything. But this I must tell you, she is also travelling with my daughter but never did she ever pay anything for daughter. Together they all three of them formed gemstone company. Then it was, she planned to return to India. But only few days before coming back she had heart attack and died. Only but few days, she is so soon coming back to see me and at that time she is now gone.

'Myself and my son we set up small mission hospital in the name of this dear lady, I am telling you she was much devotee of Lord Krishna. So after this I think I must return to place where I am meeting with *sadhu*. You remember he said I would come back to him again. Now, *sadhu* is talking and he is asking me that I am sad for someone. He tells me that lesson to learn is more important to learn than sadness. He is giving me this '*asheerwadi*' or blessing, he is telling me "Be Happy".'

Chaturvedi becomes quiet; he has come to an end. I am grateful for his sharing this very personal story.

Making my way gently through Swargashram village, I do not stop until I reach a wayside stall, laden with mounds of beautiful ripe fruits. I watch as the fruit vendor sprinkles the fruits with water from a brass pot - he has decorated his stall with freshly picked flowers. Hanging over a wall beyond his stall trail branches of flowering *Bougainvillea* and *Himalayan Red Rhododendron.*

This morning **I walk slowly**, not just because it is hot but also because **I am not in a hurry**. I am enjoying **everything** I see. Today I am happy just to let the day unfold, naturally. Without effort I climb the steep path leading up to the *dandi swami's kutir*.

'Hello, hello, how are you?' a cheeky faced pretty little child calls to me from behind the wire fence. She smiles and giggles as I reply to her in tourist Hindi. From some way off comes a man, dressed neatly in white shirt and neatly pressed brown trousers, whom I take to be her father.

Though his face is altogether unfamiliar, his questions are not.

'Where you are coming from?' he asks, his dark eyes scrutinising me. He appears suspicious, ill at ease.

'You mean my country? England,' I answer briefly. I suspect he is hoping for far more detailed information. Perhaps he thinks I am a journalist, come here to spy on him.

'You are doctor? Or businessman? Or *yoga* teacher?'

The two of us chat awhile, and as we talk we walk about the grounds here, down the wide paths overhanging with jungle trees. My companion does not appear to want to be seen by me as a common squatter, for he takes time to impress upon me that he works here, taking care of 'initiation work' (initiation being a term used by the TM organisation to mean instruction in meditation). In addition to teaching TM, he also claims to be dealing with 'management' (which evidently includes the dual tasks of watchdog and reception committee).

'At this time all activities are closed here,' he informs me. 'New buildings is here after one year.'

But it is all too evident to me that no construction work has yet been started. Perhaps he senses my doubts.

'Permit extension after some time,' he assures himself.

It is difficult to comprehend how anyone in authority could give permission to demolish any of these buildings, for none of them is particularly old.

'But if the buildings really are to be pulled down, what will take their place?'

'Good Vedic gardens and guest house for foreigns.'

'No longer an *ashram* then?'

'No,' he states, evidently uncomfortable at the thought.

I change the subject.

'I have come to see Dandi Swami Narayananand. He was not in his *kutir*. Do you think he is coming back soon?'

'Yes, you will be seeing him, Dandi Swami is very *guru*, he has enlightenment.' he comments rather matter-of-factly.

Wow! Enlightenment must be commonplace in these parts or for what other reason would he make such light work of the subject?

Suddenly a commotion erupts. An adult *langur* has suddenly appeared is attempting to tear the bag I'm carrying from my grasp. The cunning creature sidled up completely unnoticed. The paper bag spills open and several fruits fall to the ground.

'Wow, that was clever, he came out of nowhere!' I exclaim as the *langur* scampers away to the trees.

'Eighty-ninety monkeys here all the time. They are very criminal,' he replies informs me in a very serious and concerned tone. Only with difficulty do I stifle my instinct to laugh out loud.

We have arrived at a red and white-pinnacled structure, which contains a Shivalinga, a shrine to Shivashakti. Here my companion shyly asks me to take a photograph of himself and his daughter, a request I readily agree to. As they stand posing, a young woman emerges from a nearby building and steps forward into the bright sunlight. She is evidently the little girl's mother. She very quickly declines her husband's request for her to join them in the photograph, and excuses herself saying she instead wishes to perform *puja* (a religious ceremony), and she slips away. So, father and daughter pose beside the sacred *lingam* and when they are ready, the camera clicks and whirrs successfully, however, I am concerned to notice that the batteries are running extremely low. To conserve their energy, I take no more pictures, and put away the camera in my shoulder bag.

'Perhaps the *swami* has by now returned,' I suggest. 'I think I will check one time more before I go.'

'Yes, we go to him now. I think he is returned. Maybe.'

Leaving the *ashram* compound, we walk together to the gate adjacent to the holyman's rooms. I do not see anyone there, but the door to the *kutir* is ajar and a pair of sandals lies there beside it, which suggests he is back. There is a flicker of light and all-at-once the orange robed *swami* is standing directly before us. He beckons us, his bright eyes flashing a greeting of welcome. Again I am awed to be in his presence, for he radiates such a concentrated atmosphere of inner strength and well-being.

My companion speaks, telling the *swami* of the photography session. I wonder at him, that he bothers to share such information with the holyman.

When the *swami* hears tell of the photo-shoot he communicates to me by gestures that I ought to note my companions contact details. A very practical suggestion, if I am to send a copy of the printed photograph when the film has been developed. With his permission I use the *swami's* pen to take down the man's address. Swami Ji is quick to note that the address I am given by the man (Mr. Thakur), lacks a 'pin number', a postal code. Swami ji writes this for me on his chalkboard and holds it aloft, chuckling to himself as he does so. He appears to takes an almost childlike delight in involving himself in the world of administration; Mr. Thakur's designated work.

As I am still holding the pen, I think to take the opportunity to commit the holyman's likeness to paper and attempt to make a sketch of him. As I draw, I listen to Mr Thakur, who translates the Hindi words on the *swami's* chalkboard into English.

'Swami Ji, silence he makes for four months. At this time he will speak after two days.'

'Swami is also saying he knows you before,' Mr. Thakur then says, sounding very surprised and puzzled.

Well, I assume the *swami* is referring to our prior meeting, though I am not certain, for in India it is not uncommon for people to casually refer to former lifetimes! I contemplate this truth as I continue to draw the swami's likeness.

But soon I abandon my crude sketch and surprise myself as I summon up the courage to ask if I might use my camera instead. Narayananand Ji chuckles and casually unties his topknot, letting fall a shower of long silvering hair to tumble over his shoulders. Taking up the long cloth-covered '*dandi*' staff he then seats himself cross-legged on the wooden bench and motions for Mr. Thakur to pull up a chair, which he does, joining him for the photograph. The camera whirrs, the job is done. Mr Thakur does not stay.

Left alone with the *swami* I am tempted to stretch my luck a little and ask if I can take one more photo. Again he chuckles, twinkles his eyes and waggles his heavily bearded head in assent.

As he sits, he presents the definitive image of the cheery self-realised *guru*. In an instant I imagine his taking to the stage at a rock music venue - imagining the crowds taking to him very easily. I feel inspired to move my position, to crouch down in front of him. And there I compose the picture; taking care to include his wooden *paduka* sandals.

The shaded scene is dappled with morning sunlight, all that is needed is but a bounce of flash though, and I am concerned that the battery is rather too weak to power up the flash. And I fear I might be testing the *swami's* patience in keeping him waiting. I hold fire for just a while longer, raise my eyes from the camera and look to the *swami*. Swami Ji flickers his eyebrows, apparently signalling his approval that the time is right.

Pressing the button my instincts tell me the photograph is... PERFECT.

I put away the camera, get up and return to the *swami's* side, to place beside him my offering of fruits and the few flowering purple blooms that formerly adorned the street vendor's barrow. The *swami's* hands hover over the fruits a moment, as if in blessing. He gestures for me to sit on the blanket that he spreads by his side.

As I sit quietly with him my mind flickers and splutters into liveliness, I become awake to the very great opportunity this meeting affords me, for it is not everyday one has the chance to sit in the presence of such a man. I suspect that whatever people mean by the words 'enlightened' and '*guru*', he personifies them.

I begin asking him a few questions: -

'Swami Ji, should I continue my meditations?'

He responds with an affirmative roll of his head. This surprises me for I half expected that he would advise me to perform some different practice instead. On a previous visit to India I met with another monk of Jyotir Math monastery who appeared quite offish about the need for inner

meditation, saying 'Here it not necessary to meditate.' Also, when I sat for meditation in Trottacacharya Gupha, a cave near to the monastery, a monk there also voiced certain discouragement about the practice of meditation, which surprised me greatly, bearing in mind that Maharishi claims to be of the tradition of monks associated with the Jyotir Math monastic tradition.

'I also wish to teach meditation, is this alright?'

Again the *swami* offers a very positive reaction.

From his graceful responses to my earnest enquiries I derive incredible strength and support for my spiritual aspirations, and find my self-assurance is growing by the moment. As I sit glowing with the satisfaction at having gained the *dandi swami's* permission and approval, the memory of my recent hands-on healing treatment springs to mind. Without hesitation I decide to ask his opinion about such practices.

'Recently I have been given Reiki,' I explain. 'I would like to show you what happened.'

I now lie myself down prone on the trodden earth before him and proceed to re-enact some of the more sensational aspects of the session; the twists, turns, jerks and sudden bursts of rapid deep breathing. As I replay the dramatic highlights of the session he responds with nods, smiles and rolls his head from side to side. When I have finished my re-enactment he demonstrates for me a breathing exercise, indicating that it will be useful for me to practice. Drawing myself up, I practice by his example and then remain sitting cross-legged before him, assuming the role of pupil.

I have observed that *gurus* seem always seem to seat themselves higher than their visitors do, I had thought it customary for them to do so.

By gestures the *swami* makes it obvious that he does not wish for me to remain seated at his feet, but that I should return to my place beside him on the rug he has laid for me there. I return without delay. I feel no desire to speak further, since, as he has answered my questions, there is nothing better to do other than sit in the quietness and enjoy the gift of his graceful smiling companionship. After some long time spent enjoying blissful moments with the Swami Ji I notice his manner subtly alters and he now raises his strong eyebrows and for a moment the bright red *tilak* and horizontal lines of sandalwood that grace his brow almost resemble a frown. Springing to his feet he takes up a piece of cloth and, with skilful slight of hand worthy of a seasoned conjurer, he deftly uses it to cover and gather up my offerings. Whereupon, a thwarted bandit monkey scampers away to regain the cover of the jungle, it's schemes foiled again.

'What should I do next?' I ask the *swami*, hoping for some last spiritual guidance before leaving him. Without a moment's hesitation he takes up his chalkboard and writes in clear sweeping motions. My eyes light on three words in particular: -

'*Snan lata kumbh*' - *snan lata* I take to refer to bathing, *kumbh*, I vaguely recall as meaning a pot. He therefore appears to be advising me to undertake some sort of ritual bath. Perhaps he is advising me to become an ascetic?

'Where must I go?' I ask of him.

'Prayag,' he writes. Prayag I know is the term for the meeting of two rivers as found in local placenames such as Devaprayag and Rudraprayag, which I have visited. It is also the ancient name for the city of Allahabad.

'Allahabad?' I query.

He grins almost conspiratorially, as if divulging a great secret.

'Brahma Nivas, Alopi Bhag,' he writes. It is clear now, for the name of the monastery and its address are contained in an area of my memory, which has suddenly, became activated. Swami Narayanand is inviting me to go to the monastery in Allahabad

'Shankaracharya Ashram!' I marvel.

He smiles, waggles his head and nods again, crinkling his eyes, squeezing rays of his inner light to scatter about him.

I ask him when I should travel to Allahabad.

This time he uses no chalkboard, only he uses his eyes and simple hand gestures. Circling with his finger he points first to his own head and then to mine. I understand, at least I think I understand. I believe he means me to think about it. It is for me to decide.

As I stand ready to leave, he bids me wait a moment and goes to select a piece of fruit, which he presents to me. As on my previous visit, when I depart I reach to touch his feet and as I do so I feel his hands linger behind my head. As he blesses me, I hear a sound issue from him, similar to the sound of the hissing of a snake. Then again all is silent. Respectfully I bow my head and place my hands together.

'*Jay Shri Gurudev*,' I say, meaning 'Glory be to blessed Gurudev', a customary greeting in praise of his *guru*.

I back away from his presence and as I do so I notice his eyes appear to narrow slightly. But as I fervently desire one last look into the infinite depths his wide-open eyes, I pause longer, expectantly. Although I believe he understands my unspoken wish, he remains steadfast without movement, offering to me a last silent instruction - that, for whatever reason or however well intentioned, it is futile to attempt the exertion of one's own willpower over that of an enlightened master.

Chapter Nine

'Thoughts are no more than gentle vibrations moving in the ether.'

- Swami Paramahansa Yogananda

With a lightness of step, I take the descent down the steep path from Shankaracharya Nagar hill quickly. Realising that I have no further plans for the day, I make a snap decision to again walk in the jungle. The certain knowledge that I have, in my camera, a perfect image of an enlightened man excites me immensely. I resolve to walk to Rishikesh town and have the film developed this very day, but as there are more than two-dozen unexposed frames left in the camera I begin wildly pressing the button and recording wayside views.

Although it is but mid-morning the day has become hot, and with the brisk pace of my walk I become very thirsty. Having no handy carton of juice, I elect instead to enjoy the apple the *swami* has given me as *prasad*, a perfectly tasty fruit literally dripping with refreshing juice. But I eat no more than a third of the delicious gift before I realise I now have a companion walking by my side, eager for a share of the apple. Then comes another and another and soon there are several *langur* gathered around me. Using my thumbs to break the apple apart, I offer the eager creatures pieces of fruit from my outstretched hands, taking care not to let any of them take more than his fair share. I watch them as they bite and chew the succulent fruit.

Wiping my hands, wet with the apple juice, my attention falls on somebody seated a little way off, garbed in the orange cloth of renunciation. He beckons me over to a clearing under some trees where he has made a simple camp. All the while he fixes me with a smiling but extraordinarily powerful gaze and announces in a strong voice.

'I have been with you since you arrived.'

In *'Autobiography of a Yogi'*, author Paramahansa Yogananda tells of many meetings where he met with extraordinary souls. Instinctively, I know this man before me has a depth of perception far exceeding the norm. I eye his strangely intense face framed with wild shock of white hair and charcoal grey beard.

'You are feeding Hanuman monkey. This is good,' he declares happily.

He bids me join him, to sit with him upon a blanket on the dry earth. As I make myself comfortable the old man stares deeply into my eyes and as he holds up a wagging finger in front of my face, he tells me in very solemn tones: -

'You - do - not - need - to - take - permission!'

'No?' I ask, shocked that he appears to know the gist of my meeting with the *dandi swami*.

'No. You are not needing to take permission from anyone!' he repeats, almost as he is admonishing me.

I have walked briskly without delay from Swami Narayananand's *kutir*, so there can be no question of trickery or collusion. Actually though, I entertain no doubt concerning these *swamis*' gifts of skills which appear to me to surpass any offered by modern telecommunications. Stunned, I wait to find out whether he has any further revelations to make. But it appears that, having passed on these messages, the old man now feels free to relax his stance. Grinning at me he now asks the normal questions so frequently demanded of tourists concerning country and name. I am happy to tell him anything he wishes.

I am still buzzing with exuberance from my meeting with the *dandi swami* and am very eager to interpret the meaning of his advice concerning a ritual bath.

'I have just been with Dandi Swami Narayananand, he wrote these words for me, "*snan lata kumbh*",' I reveal.

The old man shows no sign of surprise.

Raising his long index finger, he waves it before my face. He rocks from side to side, leans forward and begins to explain to me, very slowly and forcefully: -

'You take bath at Kumbh Mela, this is to wash away *karma* of past lives. This special Kumbh Mela, at Prayag, only every one and half thousand years is.'

'When is Kumbh Mela?

He does not answer me immediately but continues to stare deeply into my eyes. I feel an intense bond of friendship and love for the old man. He smiles indulgently, opens his mouth and laughs the laugh of one without any real cares. Again he rocks to and fro and raises his finger, as if to announce his intention to speak.

'Jan-ua-ry second to twentieth, Jan-ua-ry second to twentieth,' he repeats. It is as if he is listening to the message and repeating it out loud for my benefit.

As I weigh up his words I sense that an important piece of my personal spiritual jigsaw is slotting into place. But I am alarmed, for an invitation to attend this very special Kumbh Mela, a religious festival to be held in Allahabad, entails not only travelling the distance of some several hundred miles, but many, many more.

'Oh, but I should be back in England in January.'

The old man now becomes very, very serious. He rocks back and forth and points up above him.

'Doing the *guru's* work is not easy. It is most difficult work,' he states, very emphatically, tilting his head.

Guru's work? Am I being tested? But who have I ever taken to be my *guru*? Only have I sometimes asked advice and information from those I have believed to be wiser than myself.

In this moment I entertain the real possibility that Swami Brahmananda (also known as 'Gurudev'), a man some fifty years departed from this earth is orchestrating events on this bright sunny day in Northern India. Did he have some hand in my getting my *sannyasi* name from Shiv Balak?

Could these apparently enlightened old holy men in point of fact really be agents of Gurudev? Is it really possible, I wonder?

'What is your name?' I ask (the detective in me coming to the fore).

'Roopanand.'

'Swaroopanand?' I check, for Swami Swaroopanand is the name of one of the few remaining disciples of Gurudev.

'Roopanand, Roopanand' he corrects me.

I sit, attentive but silent.

'So! What is my name?' he asks. He asks in such a way as to suggest I might have to dig deep deep inside my being for the correct answer.

'Swami Roopanand Saraswati Maharaj Ji,' I reply without really thinking.

'Good. This is good,' he responds with a hearty laugh.

It is difficult not to like him, to love this old man. He appears to me both rogue and saint. In his manner he is so profoundly different to the *dandi swami*, yet he exudes a lightness, a profound inner serenity.

'What do you want from me?' he now asks.

I am surprised by his question. But, strangely, I feel I might ask him for anything and he would be able to give it.

In a flash I realise that I am, at least for this moment, entirely without desires.

'I want for nothing,' I answer truthfully.

His smile wanes, he becomes particularly intense.

'So now what do you say then?' he says staring deeply into my eyes without blinking. I stay silent.

'What - you - say - now?' he repeats slowly, dramatically.

My head becomes a whirr of activity but without any resultant thought. Spontaneously I feel a sentence forming.

'Is there anything I can do for you?' I offer.

'Ah good. This is good. But I do not want money,' he says very earnestly, wagging his finger again. Suppressing my relief, I watch and wait patiently for him to continue. He speaks slowly 'I would like to come back with you, to your country, to England.'

'Oh!' I exclaim, dumbfounded. I shrink back in embarrassment, for this is worse than being asked for money, much worse. He raises his eyebrows as he awaits my reply. Confused and cornered by him I offer a weak response, saying: - 'Oh this is difficult. I must think about it.' I pray he will not raise the topic again.

Leaning down over the smouldering wood fire he takes some ash on his fingers and applies it to my forehead, slowly and deliberately creating the marks of his faith.

'This **vibhuti** - in Hindi,' he tells me, pointing to the ash.

The smears of *vibhuti* on my brow seem to cool my head, they seem to refresh my mind, helping me relax and settle down.

'Shiva eyes - Vishnu body - Brahma mind,' he explains, clarifying that the three principle Hindu deities are all located within the human body.

It is apparent that I have, without asking, become his student. He fixes me directly with his eyes, and sings: - '*Gurur Brahma, Gurur Vishnuah, Guru Devo Maheshvara.*' I am struck how very coincidental it is that he is reciting these very words of *puja*, that I have lately been fretting to remember. He recites them slowly to my face, clearly wishing me to memorise each and every word perfectly. I repeat the *puja* to his satisfaction, whereupon he shakes his head this way and that and nods approvingly.

'Rama is embodiment of God! - Hanuman is service!' he is moved to observe, throwing some food to a visiting *langur* monkey. I am aware that in the mind of the ascetic, all thoughts and actions are offered up in the service of God. The monkey Hanuman's devotion to his god-king Rama is seen as example for those on the *bhakti* or devotional path, those in service of God.

Roopanand now moves very, very close to me and again he raises his finger. It is as though he is running though a list of topics he must sort out with me.

'Only one meal eat in day. Only three hours sleep enough,' he announces.

'Yes, that's right!' I answer in astonishment. Without apparent effort he makes this accurate inventory of the new habits I have acquired since arriving in India. How does he do it, I wonder?

'You smoke?' he asks suddenly, his hand dropping and lowering to his side. Perhaps his question is just to test me. He has done it again for I am on the verge of quitting my habit of smoking cigarettes. But, something tells me he is about to offer me a *chillum* pipe.

'*Chillum nahin*,' I murmur. I wonder if he smokes hashish himself. What need would he have for drugs? Staring inquisitively into my eyes he smiles benevolently. He emanates an air of self-sufficiency and good humour.

'Where are you getting this?' he asks pointing at the cotton bracelet on my wrist.

'At the temple above Neelkanth Mahadev.'

'Good, good. Neelkanth is temple of god Shiva.'

He starts singing again, this time it is a song of devotion in praise of the god.

On the ground beside him I notice a prayer book of hymns to Lord Shiva, I ask him to translate some verses for me.

Turning over the pages he selects a passage; perhaps it is one of his personal favourites: -

'Be father, mother, brother. No problems will be. Do service.'

He then encourages me to read it for myself and I try, stumbling through a few lines of Sanskrit.

'You, every day, study Hindi! You do?' he encourages.

'Yes, I will make sure I do that.'

'Yes, yes. Every day you are Hindi language work doing. Myself I am knowing three language,' he says holding three fingers together. 'Hindi, Sanskrit and the secret language.'

The secret language?

I reflect on this disclosure. I wonder if it might hold a clue to his apparent psychic abilities. But, then I realise I have misheard him, for he must surely be referring not to the 'secret' but to the 'Sikh' language of the Punjab.

'Now,' he says, stretching and straightening his back.

By this one word he makes me understand that the lessons are finished for the day.

He asks me: - 'You have hobby?'

'I play music, guitar,' I volunteer.

'Banjo you play! This will be hobby for you.'

'Mmm. Maybe.'

'Yes, banjo you get!'

'I will try to find one,' I answer evasively.

It has been an intense exchange and I am beginning to think this might be a good time to leave. I now wish to be on my own. As I start to get up he takes hold of my knee in a powerful grip and again stares very deeply into my eyes.

'So, what you do for me?' he asks, narrowing his eyes.

I panic, realising he is again raising the subject of coming with me to England.

'Very, very difficult,' I tell him, and in Hindi repeat myself, '*Bahut bahut muskil hai*...' Then, all-at-once, a thought tumbles out in words.

'I will take you back in my heart,' I offer him.

'This is good! Very good! Yes!'. He sounds moved and impressed, as though this is the correct answer to his question, the only correct answer. It is as though I have passed a test.

He brings his face close to mine

'I know who you are!' he states with forceful conviction. Throwing the situation around. He then asks me, 'Who you are?'

Puzzled, I tell him my given name. He just stares.

'Also I have Indian name, Premanand,' I add.

'WHO ARE YOU?' he persists.

'Mmmmm....' I mumble uncertainly.

'Narayana you are. You - are - Narayana.'

I am aware that Narayana is a name of God and therefore assume he is trying to raise in my awareness the realisation that we are all potentially divine.

'I go now *Swami Ji*,' I tell him.

'Yes, it is time,' he announces drawing himself up. He stands tall. A mysterious and powerful figure.

I falter, wondering with what words I should take my leave, not knowing how to thank him for the blessing of our meeting, or his words of wisdom and encouragement.

'You are coming here again! I will be here!' he assures me.

I do not reply but instead bow forward to touch his feet.

He blesses me.

Chapter Ten

'You sound very happy,' she says.

'Well I AM,' I admit, easily.

'Have you joined a cult or something?' she queries.

'Oh, because I sound happy and mention that I have spoken to a couple of *swami's*, then I must have joined a cult?'

'But you do sound VERY happy...! I'm glad for you though.'

Admittedly, phone calls are not the best way to relate, but from an old friend I feel I should be able to expect a more positive response. If she could see the *vibhuti* marks on my forehead, her attitude would probably be no less suspicious.

Happily, the reverse appears to be true amongst the locals for whom it is as though the ash marks single me out for preferential treatment., for not only are shopkeepers more attentive and helpful, but even whilst I'm out amongst crowds, people seem to pay me special attention, some even touching my feet! Well after I wash the ash away, the spiritual magic of the two holy men seems to cling for I continue, for a while yet, to attract an extraordinarily friendly attitude towards me.

'How much you are paying for your room?' asks the manager of a restaurant I visit in Rishikesh. After I tell him, he offers me a luxury room in his hotel at a fraction of the normal cost, well below the rate of even the most basic room locally. But, he could not know that even if he were to offer the room free of charge, I would not be tempted out of my hillside retreat, surrounded as it is by natural beauty and with such ready access to enlightened masters.

I notice that a curious phenomenon has developed, that whenever the desire to visit either of my *swami* friends arises, I find them apparently waiting, and when my commitments prevent me from visiting them, they appear on my path. I note also that neither of them asks any material thing of me, though both demand my full attention.

*

The first session of the Reiki course I enjoy immensely, and at midday we break for lunch, after which I find enough time to take a short stroll in the forest in order to meet with Swami Roopanand, who greets me with great gusto, his eyes twinkling brightly. The *swami* renews his efforts to educate me. I find his manner becoming ever more familiar and friendly; I am becoming more relaxed in his company. Lazily I contemplate the smoke rising from the smouldering wood fire, when of a sudden he brings his face close to mine. He opens his eyes wide, wide open, and tells me slowly and forcibly, his manner becoming ever more grave: - 'One day you will feed ten thousand *sadhus*, cripples and... ' Swami Roopanand pauses and points to a stump of flesh where his right arm had once been, 'And ... handicapped people.'

I have not noticed his disability before, though evidently he had lost his arm long ago.

'Yes,' I assure him, 'I would like to help.'

'You give *roti*, rice and vegetable. And also *langur* you are feeding too!' he says emphatically. It is as if he were making preparations for an imminent event, a grand feast. This suggestion, that I help towards the welfare of local people, it strikes a chord.

'For a long time now I have wanted to have enough money to make a contribution to the Baba Kamla Kamli Mission. I hope I can do it.'

He listens attentively. Rising from his rug he again marks my forehead with ash, this time telling me which fingers are used for making which marks, and he explains their symbolism. Apparently, he means for me to learn to apply these marks for myself.

I would have lingered much longer with him, looking, listening and learning, but just in time I remember that I must hasten back to the hotel to continue the Reiki course. With the old man's blessing I leave.

*

Before attempting an understanding of the principles or practices of Reiki, I am shown, by example, how important it is to be able to create a calm environment. It also becomes clear how important it is for one to attain an uncluttered mind before engaging as a conductor of healing energy. I soon realise how the 'practitioner' will be vastly more effective if he or she is centred and calm. This information seems in total accordance with the instructions given by Lord Krishna to his friend Arjuna, as recounted in the *Bhagavad Gita*, "*Yogastah kuru karmani* - Established in *yoga*, perform action".

Over the two days of the Reiki course we explore many techniques aimed at focusing and stilling the mind. During this time I imagine my mind and body are, quite naturally, becoming less clogged with stresses and strains. The process of throwing-off impurities at times becomes very evident during periods of meditation, when the knees, elbows, neck and other joints give sudden twists or jerks. Unstressing can take many forms and can occur in unforeseen and quite dramatic ways.

'Aaagh,' I gasp involuntarily, as a sudden pain sears through my right wrist. The overwhelming sensation of continuing unremitting pain causes me to tear off the heavy copper bangle I wear, which was recommended to 'draw out impurities'. But still the pain persists, worse even than before. I begin to feel panic rising within me and in desperation signal my concern to Nirmoha who promptly picks up a sharp pair of scissors and shears through the cotton strands. Though I go on massaging my wrist, the Reiki lesson continues without any mention of the incident.

It is said that the technique of hands-on healing is very ancient, indeed it is believed to be many thousands of years old. The system of Reiki is thought to originate in Tibet, though its rediscovery at the end of the 19th century is credited to Dr Mikao Usui. According to Nirmoha:- 'It is known that 2000 years ago, Jesus Christ healed many people by the laying on of hands, and that it was with his clear intention and pure mind, that he was able to perform miracle healings. His healings, however, were not miracles in the sense of magic powers that lie beyond the potential of the average man; they were healings that can come through anyone who makes himself available as a channel for Reiki energy.

Nirmoha also explains the scientific basis of Reiki healing:- 'Healing means to realign ourselves with the universe, which is made out of the universal life force, and the more attuned and refined the body / mind becomes the less possible it is for one to attract the lower vibrating frequencies. Most diseases and misalignments of the body / mind are self created through unintentional misdirection of energy. Whatever we invest our energy (attention) into, we create our reality out of. If we think negative thoughts, we attract the vibrations towards us and before we know it we will be inflicted with a body ache, or a sickness, or some sort of undesired circumstance.'

'Quantum physicists have demonstrated that the atom breaks down into pure energy. This proves that everything that exists in the universe, material and non-material, is made out of rapidly moving, particles of energy. Through inner hearing we can hear energy as sound, through inner sight we can see it as light, and through inner touch we can feel it as vibrations. These inner senses are known respectively as clairaudiency, clairvoyancy and clairsentiency. Through the imagination we uncover the reality that we are able to uncover this truth in the most tangible way possible. It is not a reality that can be grasped physically because as the quantum physicists discovered, the essence of matter is not solid.'

*

Perhaps the explanations offered in connection with the healing power of Reiki also provide some explanation for the extraordinary *siddha* powers often claimed for *yogis* and *swamis*. This topic is all the more relevant when one meets with a man who can apparently tap into the thought flow of another, who must clearly have access to a deeper reservoir of energy than is commonly available.

Roopanand Ji would unfailingly pluck out a topic currently prevailing in my mind or in the mind of anyone I might introduce to him.

I had thought to tell no one about the two Sanskrit words that sprang to mind when I first decided to share the secrets of deep meditation. Nevertheless, this does not stop 'Baba' firing these exact words at me now, the meaning of which come to my mind in an instant.

Curiously, after initially speaking to me in English, Baba now seldom talks with me in Hindi. Even when I clearly have difficulty understanding him sometimes, he seems happier that I resort to attempts at telepathy than when I seek verbal answers. Occasionally, there are others gathered about him. When Anand, his blissful *chela* (disciple) is present I ask him to translate the *swami's* words.

'Baba is telling me he knows you will come to see him today. He is looking forward to your visit. He is saying that one day you will feed many *sadhus* here, he asks that you will come and cook for them? Yes? You understand me?'

'Yes. You speak excellent English! But tell me, why doesn't he speak to me in English anymore?'

'Baba says that you understand Hindi.'

Though I fail most of the telepathic tests and fare little better with understanding his Hindi, Roopanand is not deterred. He hugs me and laughs, rattles off more sentences in Hindi and hugs me again. I cannot but love the old man very dearly; a strong bond has grown between us. I will surely take him home in my heart, as I will all the other special friends I have been making.

*

माला - *Maalaa*

As luck has it, an opportunity comes for me to make suitable offerings to my spiritual benefactors, Dandi Swami Narayananand and dear old Baba Roopanand. One morning as I am talking with a local jeweller, our conversation is interrupted by a man coming by bicycle from Rishikesh. The jeweller takes delivery of two beautiful garlands of bright orange blooms similar in size, shape and perfume to French marigolds, the '*genda*' flowers are threaded together with string.

'Can I buy garlands?' I ask.

'*Mala*! You want *mala*?'

'Yes! I have two *swami* friends. I would like to buy *malas* for them.'

'These are very special *mala*, but if you want you can have. Here, take them as gift.

'Are you sure?'

'Yes, I can get other *mala*, though they are less good quality.'

I thank him and immediately set off in the direction of the *kutir* of Narayananand, stopping first to wash in the Ganga. As I clean and refresh myself, I notice the *dandi swami* walking the path towards Swargashram. Realising that any delay might make lose me this opportunity to present him with the *mala*, I quickly dry myself, gather up the garlands and run towards him. He walks faster, much faster, than I believe is possible for a man so advanced in years (for he must be well into his eighties). But he sees me and pauses, fixing me with a questioning glance. I go to make my offering, and attempt to place the garland around his neck, but he indicates that he would prefer I place it over his outstretched forearm. I infer from this that he does not intend to wear the *mala* himself, but to later offer it elsewhere, perhaps at a temple. Without further delay the *swami* is away again and it seems to me that it is only moments later that he can be seen only as an orange blur in the distance.

I now seek out Roopanand Ji and find him easily, at his usual camping spot, and he leans forward that I might place the floral offering over his head.

I leave with his blessing.

However, some time later in the day I sense I should go to see him again and on this occasion I notice there is no sign of the *mala*. I ask him where it has gone. With flamboyant gestures he tells the story of how he placed it on a tree trunk and how the *mala* soon became lunch to a visiting cow. He laughs to recall the incident. I suspect he is probably more interested in the animal's welfare than the loss of a *mala*. Actually, Baba appears to be able to make himself understood to all manner of creatures. In a mix of language, non-language sound and gesture he calls and talks with all the animals here. The monkeys, the cows and the visiting dog all seem totally at home in his company. I am awed by this gift and Baba, sensing my deep curiosity and wonder, attempts to explain his secret: -

'If for forty days you feed the animals, the *langur*, the cows, the insects and also the life in the water, you will know their language.'

Chapter Eleven

It appears that whatever the reason is for someone to arrive within the shores of Bharat (the Indian name for India), it is difficult for them to withstand personal change. Although not all who come to Rishikesh would claim to be in pursuit of spiritual knowledge, most would admit to hearing the 'wake-up call' that India gives its visitors. This call is described in a variety of ways, usually in the form of anecdotal stories, in which travellers tell of how prejudices and preconceptions have been swept aside by some specific incident with a positive outcome. Such experiences range from the trivial to the extremely serious and more often concern honesty, trust or compassion.

Onney a disc jockey from Whitby in Northern England eagerly shares with me some of his recent brushes with fate: -

'You wouldn't believe it! When I got the rickshaw, I went off to the other side of Delhi leaving my rucksack sat on the street. I didn't realise what I'd done until we had got right across the city. I can tell you.. I was worried! I mean, I've got all my stuff in there, my camera, sound stuff, passport, my money, everything! So I got back there to Old Delhi, but of course, as you can guess, I couldn't see it anywhere. What was I to do? I mean it was gone and that was that. What could I do, it looked like a trip to the embassy was in order, but I mean this was definitely the end of my holiday. But just then this man ran up to me and began tugging at my sleeve. I told him I was looking all about for my bag and it was as though he understood. Like, I found he had the bag in his shop, he'd been waiting in the street all that time for me to come back.'

'Another thing happened when I was in Delhi. My mate, he went into a toilet in our hotel and left his money belt wrapped around a pipe. He only remembered it about half an hour later. At least five or six people must have been in there before he went back, so he was really panicked. He had to wait for someone to come out. But there it was anyway, still wrapped around the pipe, nobody had so much as touched it.

'Me, I thought everybody was only after money, they have some really clever ways of getting to you. Good deals, hard luck stories, they really get onto you, they really work on the psychology. Well I was just thinking about this when I tripped over and smashed my head open, blood all over the place. Well, this woman came over and fixed it up really nicely and you know? She wouldn't take any money! So instead I tried to buy some stuff off her stall, but she wouldn't sell me anything. Only when I told her that I really liked the stuff and I really wanted to buy some gifts for friends did she let me buy anything at all. She didn't want me to buy her stuff just for helping me out. She amazed me. It really changes your mind, I can tell you. Anything you think about them, well it turns around the other way. They're much nicer than you'd think. People back home just fill your head with fears like "You'll get sick"; "You'll get ripped off". Actually they're some of the nicest people you could ever meet!'

Scots Andy seems to get his 'wake-up' call from nature:- 'I mean we saw this snow leopard up near Ladakh, people come especially to try and find them. We were just passing though and ... there it is! That is one of the rarest sights you could ever see.'

But Andy, unlike Jane, his girlfriend, has yet to be won over to the spiritual dimension of *yoga* teachings. Whilst she has been studying, with Swami Vivekananda, a Romanian, Andy has been off on his own, unsuccessfully looking for under-the-counter eggs and black market liquor. Perhaps it's not just the claim that the Romanian has attained enlightenment that bothers him, it could also be that the *tantra yoga* taught by Vivekananda is rumoured to encompass practices more in keeping with the *Kama Sutra* than with *yoga* classes at local educational institutes back home.

Corby, one of a group freshly arrived in India from life on a Kibbutz, in Israel, although open to the possibility that spiritual practices can work for individuals, is worried that '*moksha*', 'liberation', might lead to a lack of concern about the welfare of others. Then from a local holy man he learns that *moksha* actually means death and he is astonished when the *swami*, unprovoked, lectures him upon the need for social responsibility.

Attoro, an engaging Austrian Reiki Master, long ago heard the wake-up call and now spends his time flitting from *ashram* to *ashram*, learning new techniques, enjoying chance meetings and discovering the secret powers of the mind. By some uncanny stroke of good fortune, he claims that events frequently turn to his advantage. If he has to visit Delhi, he is given five-star accommodation without charge. If he has to make an air trip it is by VIP class on a ticket a fraction of the normal cost. Attoro has been offered an intriguing clue to his good fortune:- 'My *guru* explained to me why things go like this, it is because I am a king in my last life.'

Kalidas, another Reiki Master and long-time inmate of a local *ashram* heard his wake-up call earlier than most:-

'We lived in London. I had learnt everything I know about Shamanism from my Russian mother by the time I was eight.'

After first visiting Rishikesh in the late sixties he has come to regard India as his home. To the suggestion that he might one day return to the West he retorts:-

'But I won't come back. This is where I live. I never ever leave this place, there is nowhere else I want to be.'

*

In the queue at the departure lounge at Delhi airport I shuffle along with my rucksack and my shoulder bag, taking great care to protect my most fragile belongings, such as the unusual little Indian Banjo I have acquired. I must also take care of the more sophisticated technical devices I have brought back, purchased from the music store in Dehra Dun near Rishikesh.

Whilst I wait to check in my baggage, a middle-aged Indian woman questions me on how I have spent my time in India.

'You have been to Goa? To Rajastan? You are liking India?' she asks.

'I stayed only up in Rishikesh.' I respond.

'Oh good, Rishikesh is a holy place. Our party travelled as far Hardwar; Hardwar is also Holy City. There we went for Divali. We are saying many prayers there. Myself I would have liked to go further on. Tell me, are you staying in *ashram* at Rishikesh? You are practicing *yoga*? You are doing some kind of meditation?'

I smile, wondering how best I should answer her. I do my best.

We move on further towards the baggage desk.

'Would you like to see a couple of photographs I have taken?' I ask.

'Thank you, yes!' she says eagerly.

As I show her portraits of Dandi Swami Narayananand and Baba Roopanand I notice that she visibly glows as she studies the photographs. As I watch her I tell her more about these holymen, and at the same time I fumble about in my pockets, searching for the block of treacly sweet *gur* that Roopanand pressed into my hands only hours before.

'*Prasad* from the Baba,' I say holding out the tiny cake wrapped in a scrap of newspaper. 'Take it, you can share with your friends.'

'*Dhanyavad*. Thank you,' she thrills, pressing the *gur* to her forehead, before carefully stowing it in her hand luggage.

'Where is this Baba staying?' she asks, 'Where is he?'

As I think about how best to describe where in the jungle I first met with Roopanand Ji, I stop myself, and instead simply touch myself lightly on the chest.

www.ingramcontent.com/pod-product-compliance
Lightning Source LLC
Chambersburg PA
CBHW040322300426
44112CB00020B/2844